SPEAKING OF FRIENDSHIP

Recent Titles in
Contributions in Women's Studies

American Women and Political Participation: Impacts of Work, Generation, and Feminism
Karen Beckwith

The American Victorian Woman: The Myth and the Reality
Mabel Collins Donnelly

Gender and Destiny: Women Writers and the Holocaust
Marlene E. Heinemann

Nineteenth-Century Women Writers of the English-Speaking World
Rhoda B. Nathan, editor

Women's Rights in France
Dorothy McBride Stetson

Charity, Challenge, and Change: Religious Dimensions of the Mid-Nineteenth Century Women's Movement in Germany
Catherine M. Prelinger

Woman as Mediatrix: Essays on Nineteenth-Century European Women Writers
Avriel H. Goldberger, editor

Women and American Foreign Policy: Lobbyists, Critics, and Insiders
Edward P. Crapol, editor

From Ladies to Women: The Organized Struggle for Woman's Rights in the Reconstruction Era
Israel Kugler

Unlikely Heroines: Nineteenth-Century Women Writers and the Woman Question
Ann R. Shapiro

Beyond the Public/Domestic Dichotomy: Contemporary Perspectives on Women's Public Lives
Janet Sharistanian, editor

Speaking of Friendship

MIDDLE-CLASS WOMEN AND THEIR FRIENDS

Helen Gouldner
and Mary Symons Strong

Contributions in Women's Studies, Number 80

GREENWOOD PRESS
New York • Westport, Connecticut • London

Library of Congress Cataloging-in-Publication Data

Gouldner, Helen.
Speaking of friendship.
(Contributions in women's studies, ISSN 0147-104X ; no. 80)
Bibliography: p.
Includes index.
1. Women—Psychology. 2. Middle class women—United States—Psychology. 3. Friendship—United States. 4. Interpersonal relations. I. Strong, Mary Symons. II. Title. III. Series.
HQ1206.G73 1987 305.4'2 86-29407
ISBN 0-313-25068-5 (lib. bdg. : alk. paper)

Library of Congress Catalog Card Number: 86-29407
ISBN: 0-313-25068-5
ISSN: 0147-104X

First published in 1987

Greenwood Press, Inc.
88 Post Road West, Westport, Connecticut 06881

Printed in the United States of America

The paper used in this book complies with the Permanent Paper Standard issued by the National Information Standards Organization (Z39.48-1984).

10 9 8 7 6 5 4 3 2 1

To Our Friends

Contents

Acknowledgments

We wish to express our indebtedness to the women whose interviews about their friendship experiences provided the data for this study. Each one of them made an important contribution to expanding our knowledge of the meaning of friendship in women's lives.

We are grateful for the assistance of a number of other individuals. L. Leon Campbell, Provost and Vice President for Academic Affairs at the University of Delaware, encouraged a fellow administrator to undertake the study and secured financial support for its completion. David Riesman was always generous in sharing his insightful responses to early drafts of some of the chapters. Mary Howard and Judy Briggs made valuable criticisms of several sections of the manuscript. Dorothy Sterrett and Arlene Henry gave skillful and untiring secretarial assistance. Over the years many other colleagues and friends sustained us through their interest and support.

SPEAKING OF FRIENDSHIP

CHAPTER 1

Introduction

Speaking of Friendship is about the friendships of middle- and upper-middle-class American women. It is based on interviews with seventy-five women between the ages of thirty and sixty-five. Asked to participate in a study of adult women's friendships, virtually all the women who agreed to be interviewed were not only willing to talk about their friendships, but also wanted to discuss them at great length. "I don't know why I'm telling you all this," one of the women said. "I've never mentioned that thought to anyone before, aren't you surprised?" This with no pause for an answer. "I don't know if you're interested in the details of the start of my friendship with two other women who are closer to each other than I am to them. I have some ideas about this that I think we should return to later." When later has become two hours the interviewer suggests that it has been an enormously valuable session and perhaps the interviewee is tired. "Well, we could stop for now and pick it up after dinner" is the reply. It's touch and go whether the dinner will ever be put on the table. Friendship can be sufficient food for thought and nourish a long and probing—usually emotional—discussion.

On the subject of friendship, the women taking part in the study had a great deal to say and a great readiness to explore the subject with another woman. This eagerness to discuss their experiences with friendship was shared equally by the women who had close friends and those who did not. One of the latter said, "Yes, I have dozens of acquaintances," and added quickly, "but not one real friend. I don't have someone I can go to and sit down with and say, 'I feel terrible. I've got to talk about it.' I used to go and plunk my feet up on my sister's kitchen table and talk, but she's moved away. I have my husband and I'd say we've become each other's best friend, but I miss having a woman as a close friend. . . . I don't know why. I'd like to understand that better."

Like this woman, a number of the respondents took the opportunity provided by the interview to examine ways they had conducted their friendships and to assess the quality of their relationships with friends during their adult years. Being forced to part with their female friends was a common and upsetting feature of this experience. Virtually all the women had been through disruptions in the continuity of the relationships with friends in the course of a series of changes of residence by themselves or their friends. Their husbands' and their own professional and management careers had involved both social and geographical mobility, and these moves had periodically unsettled the composition of their personal network of friends. Separation from old friends had precipitated a search for new friends. The outcome of a woman's efforts to make friends in a new setting and to replace those who moved away was problematic. Sometimes it worked out well; other times it was less satisfactory. The history of the friendships of these women bore the distinctive stamp of the mobile social and occupational class to which they belonged.[1]

In sharp contrast to the middle class, members of the working class are far less mobile, and kin are predominant in their personal relationships. Their lives are embedded in extended family relationships that provide continuous and stable sets of support and companionship. Unlike the middle class, working-class families usually live near and associate principally with family members and old friends throughout their lives. They prefer it that way. When asked to state where they would choose to live once they are married, working-class women indicate that they want to stay close enough to "family" to allow for easy visiting back and forth. This does not mean that they would necessarily select a house across the street from their parents or in the same block with other relatives. Living that close to relatives invites the possibility of too much interference in their lives by the older generation. But they do manage to settle in locations that enable them to drop in often and spend spare time with one another.

Female relatives in the working class often become closest friends and confidantes. Of course not every pair of female relatives in the working class is necessarily compatible. Selections of preferred companions are made among available relatives. "I like my sister-in-law the most," one woman says. "She's kind of gabby and puts me at ease. I'm kind of quiet—but around her it seems like I talk more and enjoy myself." Another woman likes to "pal around" with her favorite aunt and an old girlfriend. A third explains, "I like my mother most. She's always ready to pick up and go shopping with me. . . . We go out nearly every morning, then she comes home for lunch with me" (Rainwater, Coleman, and Handel 1961, 114). However, whatever the choice, wives and sisters of blue-collar workers spent the better part of their free time with female relatives whom they regarded as friends; mothers or sisters were the usual confidantes (Komarovsky 1962).

The sheer availability of relatives and neighborhood friends of longstanding permits the sharing of everyday lives. Affection and services flow easily among them. As parents age, the younger generation helps them out financially and in doing chores, such as household repairs and shopping, while parents in turn assist with babysitting and other services that they can supply personally (Adams 1970). Over the years the composition of their primary attachment systems remains virtually intact. Easy access, familiarity, and continuity are the hallmarks of the American kin-centered working-class sociability.

The organization and composition of the sociable relations of middle-class women differ rather dramatically from this established network of family ties that are inherited by working-class women. The kinship component in the social networks of modern middle-class women seems to be waning (Bernard 1981). It is not only that geographical separation from the family circle forces middle-class women to find other people to associate with and befriend, but that independence from parental bonds and individuality are highly valued in middle-class culture. This is not to suggest that ties to parents are severed by grown children. It is generally agreed that married children from middle-class backgrounds in both the United States and Britain are active in keeping up relationships with their parents and siblings, even when physically separated from them (Bott 1971). However, although there is genuine concern for each other's well-being, visiting with family members is not done with the same emphasis on enjoyment and relaxation as it is with friends.

When a sample of middle-class women ranging in age from young to elderly was asked to list their five best friends, for example, relatives constituted only 25 percent of those named as close friends (Candy, Troll, and Levy 1981). It is logical to expect that the many new elements in middle-class women's lives—their advanced education, continuous employment, demanding jobs, later marriage, fewer children—will not only change their attitudes, values, and life styles, but also influence their repertoire of relationships. Family members are increasingly likely to develop in highly individualized ways and, consequently, to have less in common than colleagues and associates pursuing similar tracks of development.

Young women often look to friends of their own age and circumstances for counsel and support rather than to relatives, and the older generation of middle-class women find that in many respects, they, too, gain more satisfaction from friendships with their own contemporaries rather than with family members (Bernard 1981). Although it is gratifying to feel securely embedded in a caring kinship structure in the later years, older women also appreciate being able to escape from the nurturing roles so often expected of mothers and grandmothers. They like to associate with equals who have been chosen voluntarily on the basis of personal attraction rather than obligation. "Because friendship rests on mutual choice and mutual need and involves a voluntary exchange of sociability between equals, it sustains a person's sense of usefulness and self-esteem far more effectively than filial relationships" (Blau 1973, 67).

The frequent moves made by middle-class Americans accelerate both the formation of new friendships and the loss of old ones. Leaving home and familiar childhood scenes takes place in mid-adolescence of college-bound youth from middle-class families who consider sending their children away for their higher education an important aspect of their emancipation—the American rite of passage. Getting an education and starting a career frequently entail going to places far from home, with resulting disruptions and subsequent loss of some earlier relationships. It is, consequently, a rather common experience—beginning in late adolescence and early adulthood—to give up important relationships when physical interaction is no longer possible. Among the respondents to a *Psychology Today* survey about friendship, for example, a majority of whom were middle-class women under thirty years of age, moving was the reason most frequently given for the termination of their friendships (Parlee 1979).

Throughout their adult lives many women start from scratch to seek out and cultivate a new set of friends in a number of different places and circumstances. In the course of doing this, they give up their local network of personal relations. "We live in a society that is constantly on the move as we follow careers to new cities and towns, distancing ourselves from family members and often not staying in one place long enough to form great, long-lasting friendships. . . . You don't hear much about family friendships that span nearly two decades these days, but when it occurs it is a treasured gift" (Mann 1985).

MIDDLE CLASS IMAGES OF FRIENDSHIP

For middle-class Americans, friendship—much like marriage—is a highly romantic concept. But compared with the feelings about marriage and all the doubts about its survival, friendship has, if anything, been increasingly idealized, at least in the popular literature. Friendship, it is believed, can be the best of relationships because it is free; it can be entered into voluntarily by people for the sheer joy of it. It can be engaged in and terminated without legal entanglements or institutional obligations.

Americans use the term "friend" rather loosely. It is not unusual, for example, for them to refer to their neighbors, colleagues at work, members of their social clubs and organizations, and intimates alike as "friends." Most people, on reflection, differentiate with more degrees of precision between acquaintances and friends—and their shallow and their deep friendships. And some put a good deal more stock in friendship than do others. But on the whole, Americans, especially those in the middle class, are apt to apply the term to so many types of relationships that they include most of their acquaintances under the canopy of friendship.

It has often been said that Americans are an especially open and friendly people. If this characterization is meant to describe in part their usual outlook on the desirability of making a pleasant social life with friends and having some close friends, the generalization is probably accurate. At the same time, "Americans appear to hold contradictory attitudes and sentiments about friendship. At one extreme there is the idealization of friendship as a totally involving relation of great closeness, able to meet most, if not all, of the emotional and social needs of the partners. At the other extreme Americans explain . . . that such a relation cannot really exist in modern society . . . because of the constraining measures on adults in the middle years of life" (Lopata 1981, 1-2).

In their relations with associates who are not members of their immediate families, middle-class Americans seem to be caught between still other conflicting imperatives. On the one hand, there is the expectation of easy sociability expressed in the need to put on the appearance of cordiality—the mechanical smiles, the ready handshaking, the quick embrace and kissing on the cheek, the friendly persona of the other-directed, the charming, engaging persons adept at gathering around themselves an attentive circle of equally charming friends (Riesman 1950). Side by side with this goes the opposite cultural imperative that rejects the superficiality of too-easy affability, is repelled by the role of the ugly American salesman-receptionist. This imperative expresses itself in the need to cultivate "meaningful" deep relationships with just a few others.

Whichever imperative is acted on—and many attempt to embrace both of them at once—there is a great longing for friendship, an emotion that the culture "out there" reinforces at every turn by the way the system is organized and what its public media broadcast about the good life. But what the culture defines as desirable and the individuals in it want for themselves can often be elusive. Getting friends and enjoying friendship are far from automatic achievements. Part of the problem is that it is unclear what being a friend and having a friend consist of. One frequent response to the uncertainty is the tendency to try to upgrade friendships, to romanticize them, and, as one observer put it, "to elevate what others see as a casual acquaintanceship to friendship, and friendship to close friendship. . . . It is as if friendship is an artifact of desire, a wish relationship, a private agreement between two people to act 'as if' rather than to have a real relationship between two persons" (Liebow 1969, 207).

Realizing how enthusiastic people are about the abstract idea of friendship, it is necessary to be on guard when listening to what they have to say about their own experiences with it. People so much want that "comfort, the inexpressible comfort of feeling safe with a person," pictured so blissfully by George Eliot, that they will quite unintentionally describe their friendships unrealistically. When pairs of friends are interviewed separately, for example, it is startling to discover the extent of the mutual misconceptions of their regard for each other. One woman says, "Jinny and I are very close friends. I can tell her everything and she would do anything for me," while the Jinny in question does not rank this particular woman among her truly intimate friends.

STUDYING FRIENDSHIP

Studies of friendship in the United States must proceed with great caution. Given the hopes and wishes about friendship, it is extremely difficult to get valid pictures of friendship patterns. In our study we knew that somehow we were going to have to discount the fantasies surrounding it—that tendency to speak of the mere wish for close friendship as if it were a reality. So we lined up an important caveat for ourselves, about the ideology, expectations, and hopes operating among Americans for the quality of their friendships, and for the quantity of them. (And we have to remind ourselves of this repeatedly because when the caveat goes unheeded, the research questions are wrongly put and the data dirtied by misconstructions.) The caveat is that friendship relationships among Americans sometimes have carried, and still carry, a heavy burden of self-deception and disguise. The self-deception consists of not knowing or not admitting to one's self the reality about the quality (that is, their depth or superficiality) of one's friendships. The disguise consists of hiding from outsiders and embellishing what is known to be the truth about the number and quality of one's friendships.[2] Both self-deception and disguise create enormous methodological problems for the research reported in the literature and for our own strategies for getting new data that would presumably have some claim to validity.

The self-deception and disguise, as well as the idealization of friendship, create not only methodological problems for research, but also obviously create problems for any friendship. In general, not only is friendship idealized, but the disparities between ideal and actual behavior tend to make some friendships fragile. "Conflicts may develop between high expectations placed on the friendship and the 'image of man' as basically untrustworthy" (La Gaipa 1981, 73).

We are convinced, therefore, that it is hard to get valid data about American friendships, especially if the researcher approaches people directly and head on with questions about their friendships, and especially if the study design uses survey techniques to gather the information. Here is an example of what the problem is. The well-known and highly respected Detroit Area Study, which for many years has been conducting periodic interviews of a random sample of white males between the ages of twenty-one and sixty-four, included in their mid-1970s survey some questions about the respondents' friends, along with a whole battery of other questions (Stueve and Gerson 1977). The men were asked to name the three men they felt closest to and saw most often, and then they were asked about the characteristics of those friends and friendships. What would any man do if he were asked these questions? He would supply the answers, and all gave detailed information about their three closest friends—who they were, and when, where, and how often they were together. The problem was that when these men were asked a leading question about their friends, they were likely to be obliging about answering it and certainly not apt to say to the interviewer with the structured questionnaire, "Well, to tell you the truth, I don't really have any close friends. I'd like to know what you mean by close friends. I have the people at the office and some good neighbors. Is that what you mean by close friends?" Instead, the Detroit men of all ages told the interviewers that they felt "very close" to half their best friends. The younger men answered that they felt most intimate with the friends they had made early in life, while the older men said that they had made intimate friendships with men whom they had met at all stages of their lives. The claims made by the men appeared to be words put in their mouths that most of them would never use on their own to characterize their friendships.

We are skeptical about the data reported to interviewers with preset questions about friendship (Lowenthal and Haven 1968). Compare the findings of the Detroit study, for example, with what Daniel Levinson and his colleagues found in their long-term in-depth study of men passing through the stages of their careers, experiencing what were called the transitions and crises typically facing American men in mid-life. The interviewers spent many hours with each man over a period of time. In *The Seasons of a Man's Life*, Levinson wrote:

> In our interviews, friendship was largely noticeable by its absence. As a tentative generalization we would say that close friendship with a man or woman is rarely experienced by American men. This is not something that can be adequately determined by a questionnaire or mass survey. The distinction between friend and acquaintance is often blurred. A man may have a wide social network in which he has amicable, "friendly" relationships with many men and perhaps a few women. In general, however, most men do not have any intimate male friends of the kind that they recall fondly from boyhood or youth. Many men have had casual dating relationships with women, and perhaps a few complex love-sex relationships, but most men have not had an intimate, nonsexual friendship with a woman. We need to understand why friendship is so rare, and what consequences this deprivation has for adult life (Levinson, et al. 1978, 335).

So how should we approach the study of adult friendship? The literature is rich in ideas, but hard data are scarce and the findings tenuous and often conflicting. Given the burden of self-deception and disguise surrounding friendship, we felt that questionnaires and surveys were out of the question. We simply do not trust the data gathered in this way.

We hoped to get past the normative and expected accounts that so much of the survey literature on friendship has yielded. We wanted to get *more* than socially acceptable answers and to make some clearer distinctions between the kinds of friends people actually have—whether they have strong, lukewarm, or weak ties with others who are regarded as friends. What is reported of course is very much affected by what questions are asked.

We decided to focus on friendship among comfortably off American women in their adult years—a largely unexplored area of adult relationships that are not linked specifically to the family (Hess 1972). Parenthetically, it should be said that the study is not confined to friendships between women to the exclusion of their friendships with men. A number of studies have excluded other family members—a husband, mother, child—as friends, and we think that is an unfortunate omission. For one thing, it excludes the possibility that family members may be very good friends—even best friends—and the corollary of this, that some people may not have any friends to speak of beyond the family circle. In fact, we have already heard from some of the married women we've interviewed some form of expression like, "Oh, you know, I've been talking about my friends in the neighborhood and the ones in the old neighborhood we left when we last moved, but Jack is *really* my best friend." With people on the move from one job to the next, one has to be prepared to leave friends quickly and without too much regret, and possibly settle for the most enduring friendship in the person of one's spouse.

In defining the sample as American middle-class adult women between thirty and sixty-five, we wanted to narrow the age groups of the population we were studying for particular reasons. Women in their teens and twenties were not included because we were concerned with studying adult women, not those involved in their first forays into grown-up relationships and in their later attempts to establish a foothold in a career and/or become a wife/friend to a man and a mother to children. Friendship, we were sure, would have some decidedly different characteristics at earlier ages.

The Study Design

This is a qualitative investigation of women's friendships that lays no claim to representing findings about prestated variables derived from a systematically selected sample of respondents. The material used for analysis and cited in the following chapters was taken from interviews with seventy-five women who were in their thirties, forties, fifties, and early sixties. These women were included in the study by the "snowball" method of sampling. After each interview the respondent was asked for referrals. Often the names of personal friends and neighbors were suggested. Sometimes professional colleagues and business associates were recommended. This linkage between the respondents provided the opportunity to study some friendship pairs and circles of women friends.

Two of the women who were recommended by respondents refused to be interviewed. They were members of a card-playing circle that had met almost weekly for more than twenty years. In declining to participate in the study, one of them said, "What's the use of talking to me? I have nothing to add to the study. I don't have any friends." A few others agreed to be interviewed despite the painful reticence they felt about exposing their feelings of failure—the reaction they had to not having friends, or at least not having "good enough" friends. Others wanted to talk about their problems with loneliness.

The project was designed as a study of women who were middle- and upper-middle class, without pressing financial worries. They came from a variety of backgrounds and circumstances. The sample included women at home raising families and women working outside the home, some of whom were involved in demanding professional and business careers while others held run-of-the-mill female jobs. There was an assortment of married, divorced, and widowed women, singles living alone, and single heads of households. Their schooling ran the gamut of high school graduation through professional and graduate degrees as marks of educational status. The majority of the subjects resided in the cities and suburbs located along the Boston-to-Washington corridor, while a minority were from the Midwest and the West Coast.

The interviews were unstructured in-depth discussions that lasted between one and six hours, and sometimes entailed more than one session. The average interview lasted for about one and one-half hours. There were no set questions. However, the interviewer was able to guide the discussion into covering certain topics common to all the interviews. Responding to the train of thought of an individual, the interviewer tried to create a relaxed atmosphere in which the women would give free expression to their thoughts, feelings, and perceptions. It was the intention not to limit the focus of the discussion to the topic of friendship, but to encourage the respondents to indicate how their friends fitted into the rest of their social relationships. An effort was made to avoid falling into the trap of describing only so-called *true* friendship and *real* confidantes so that the actual patterns of behavior, rather than just idealized accounts of friendship, would be given. In other words, rather than defining "friendship" for the respondents, we listened to them talk about their friends, be they kin or non-kin, with the intention of learning what the reality of friendship was for them.

The interviews were recorded on tape and transcribed in full. As soon as the transcriptions were prepared, they were analyzed independently by the two researchers. Afterward their findings were compared and analyzed. Understanding all the scientific drawbacks of this methodology, we nevertheless deemed it appropriate to the subject matter, that of women's personal perceptions of their friendship experience and practices, and the meaning of friendship in their lives.

In the subjective accounts of the women's experience with friendship, the outstanding feature was the complexity of each woman's repertoire of relationships. By the time she had reached middle adulthood, she had engaged in a broad range of relationships: daughter, wife, mother, employee, and friend, just to mention a few important roles. The ties to others that had been established in these relationships had taken various forms and had different degrees of salience to her over the decades of her life. A backward glance at how her friendships had fitted into the rest of her personal attachments required her to reconstruct her past and present social networks.

It was understood that these retrospective accounts were seldom factually accurate. The very process of recollection forced each woman to be selective and indeed judgmental. As the historian of her own life story, she interpreted the development of relationships in the light of her current outlooks. What was real to a woman in the present was not necessarily true in the past. But that did not deny the reality to her of her memories, nor of her assessments made in the present. The significance of the retrospective story was that it allowed a woman to give a contemporary interpretation of her friendship experience. Consequently, the interviews were accepted as valid reflections of a woman's personal world of friendship (Stolorow and Atwood 1979).

Out of the accumulated experience of the seventy-five women as it was told in their interviews, it was possible to discern some common dimensions in the friendship process. We can venture to say something about what goes on in middle-class women's friendships: their beginnings, their maintenance and repair, their deepening to intimacy, their vicissitudes, and, sometimes, their endings. These middle-class women have made friends of many sorts and at different levels of intimacy. In the following chapters the processes of being a friend and having friends are described as a kind of natural history of women's friendships. It is intended to provide the beginnings of a guide to this uncharted, complex relationship.

NOTES

1. For empirical studies of friendships of middle-class American women, see Nona Glazer-Malbin, ed., *Old Family/New Family,* New York: Van Nostrand, 1975; Helena Z. Lopata, *Women as Widows*, New York: Elsevier, 1979; Robert R. Bell, *Worlds of Friendship*, Beverly Hills, Calif.: Sage, 1981; Jessie Bernard, *The Female World*, New York: Free Press, 1981.

2. For a further elaboration of these contradictory tendencies, see Joseph Bensman and Robert Lilienfeld, *Between Public and Private: The Lost Boundaries of the Self*, New York: Free Press, 1979.

CHAPTER 2

Beginnings: Prefriendship and Getting Acquainted

> We have lived here for five years, but for the first year Velma and I weren't friends. I didn't even meet her for quite awhile, and then it didn't happen right away. Velma said later that she realized she wasn't very neighborly in welcoming me. She says she knows she should stop by when new people move in, but she never does.

Not taking the trouble to be "neighborly" was Velma's usual way of not incurring any future social obligations to new residents of her neighborhood. As she explained later to Betsy, "There was no personal slight intended." Although a few of the suburbanites in the study reported that they still made a practice of welcoming newcomers by paying a call and bringing over coffee and sandwiches when the moving van showed up, most people were more cautious about involving themselves in beginning relationships that they might not want to pursue later on. In city apartments it could take years for residents to give some faint sign of recognition of one another as occupants of the same building. When there were unavoidable contacts, such as repeated meetings in the foyer or the elevator, they might nod and even say "Good evening" to people whose names they did not know or care to know. Averting the eyes and not speaking at all, however, were better strategies for retaining the stance of strangers.[1] When there was nothing to gain from acknowledging the existence of others and much to be lost by assuming any responsibility for returning a greeting regularly in the future, it was possible to see the same person repeatedly without making an outward gesture of recognition. As some apartment dwellers put it, "They just look right through you without batting an eye. I feel as though I'm invisible."[2]

SETTINGS AND TIMES: SOURCES OF FRIENDSHIP

Just because people were not inclined to act in a friendly manner with everyone around them, as people typically do in small towns, it did not necessarily follow that they were either friendless or lonely (Franck 1980). Friendship certainly had not ceased to exist either in the chilly urban environments or in the fenced-off suburban enclaves, or in the housing developments where a majority of the respondents taking part in the Adult Women's Friendship Project lived. The women who never spoke while riding the same elevator of their apartments and office buildings had friends living in other places—at the next subway stop, on the opposite side of town, in adjoining counties and other states, and in distant parts of the country. The residences of their friends were more apt to be dispersed geographically than located in a surrounding neighborhood where everybody knew everybody else and many of the same people shared the important events of life, from birth to death.

Although it was obviously the case that people living in physical proximity had a better chance of getting acquainted than did random pairs in the general population, neighbors were not always mentioned by the women in their rankings of their first-tier friends. In fact, in some instances their acquaintanceship with people in the immediate surroundings was so limited as to be virtually nonexistent. However, the more traditional pattern of having friendships among neighbors still persisted among the denizens of old and well-established residential sections of metropolitan areas, in outlying commuter cities, towns, and villages, and in some housing developments or condominium groups of more recent vintage (Hunter 1978). In such neighborhoods, individuals who were friendship pairs—and interlocking circles of women—had been friends for many years. Living in houses located along pleasant tree-lined streets, these friends had shared the lives of their families almost as though they were blood relatives. Although the close friends of these women—in many instances they were best friends and confidantes—could be classified as their neighbors, it was almost always true that each woman had an additional good friend or two living in another city, possibly a college classmate and a friend made in early adulthood. When neighbors were good friends, then, it did not necessarily indicate that the social ties of such women were by any means confined to what they regarded as their immediate or general neighborhood.

Friendship over the Life Cycle

During the friendship interviews the women could recall the time, the place, and the circumstances of their first meeting with each one of their good friends. Each beginning was placed in a decade of the life cycle (B. Brown 1981). Although only a few mentioned making friends in the preschool and grade school years, more spoke of having girlfriends in high school, and many were reminded of their college days, when friendships were begun while living with roommates or other occupants of a common dormitory wing—classmates assigned to live together more or less by lot who, in the course of intense interaction (for example, the bull sessions lasting through the night and the "crazy escapades"), had in time become fast friends.

In early adulthood the friendships that were made at first jobs and in early marriage and child-rearing years were of a different quality from those of childhood and adolescence (Dickens and Perlman 1981). Partings with such friends were frequent during this part of the life cycle, which typically included a decade or so of moves to new places and better jobs. After each change of residence the fabric of an established network of friends had been torn up—sometimes destroyed completely, although a selected few of the friendships left behind continued a truncated existence by telephone and periodic visits—and it was not unusual for women to keep an array of such relationships at ever-widening points of the compass. On the other hand, the act of pulling up roots and leaving familiar people and places had precipitated the loss of many friends, and these residential moves were usually followed by a hunt for new friends who could be associated with more readily than those from whom the women were spatially separated.

Other beginnings of friendship in adulthood occurred when the women had met an especially attractive person and then took the opportunity to add to an existing network of casual and close friends—and sometimes this happened when they had felt the need to replace a flagging friendship with a new relationship. However, not all efforts at making new friends during these years resulted in establishing the kinds of relationships the women desired. Some women had tried repeatedly to make new friends without success and felt discouraged about the poor quality of their social lives. A few had become rather cynical about human relations and expressed bitter feelings about how others had misled them into thinking they could count on their friendships and then had let them down. A number of these women felt isolated and quite lonely (Lopata 1973).

The majority of the women, however, were either moderately or highly satisfied with most of their friendship experiences, even though they had also been through some periods of less satisfaction. The accounts of the beginnings of their friendships—when they could be recalled in any detail—revealed how effectively almost all of them had responded to the conditions of the peculiar social and physical habitats of this affluent sector of American society. Over the decades of their lives these women in their thirties, forties, fifties, and sixties had entered a number of complex environments and had managed to make them livable. This did not mean they had never known "down times" in their social relationships during transition periods. They all knew the meaning of loneliness. A few had never overcome the difficulties of living in what has been called "a nation of strangers."[3] In general, however, the women in our sample understood that they had to use their own resources—both psychological and financial—if they were to cope with the realities of existence in a complex world. Some measure of initiative was required if they were to be successful at acquiring the number and kinds of personal relationships that were satisfying—not too few, not too many.

In their recollections of the beginnings of their friendships, it was evident that most of them had accumulated a fund of personal wisdom about initiating relationships. They could explain what had worked for them and what had not. It was clear that women had different requirements for sociability outside the family. Most of them had taken an active stance toward the tasks of creating the kinds of social relationships that they wanted, and in many cases they seemed to have applied themselves purposefully to establishing a minicommunity consisting of various types of acquaintances, casual associates, and close friends. At various periods of their lives this had involved them in trying to replace their network of friends after residential relocations and an assortment of other changes in their personal lives.

At some point, however, their geographical mobility appeared to come to a stop, or at least to a long pause, and they no longer needed to explore new avenues for interesting contacts. Even so, a good deal of turnover in a woman's complement of relationships was likely to take place even after she had settled into a residence for the long term. Changes in the composition of her social network continued to happen throughout her adult life. Such a change might come to pass when an old friend moved, thereby emptying a slot for a new occupant. At this more settled stage the job of replacing lost friends was not regarded as an easy or routine undertaking, since it was so often brought about by a painful separation from an old friend who had contributed some special meaning to daily life. Unlike family members, friends were not supplied automatically, so it put the burden on the individual women to take an active role in befriending women and in responding to the overtures of other women. No longer expected to keep close to home and neighborhood—as much as women once were—they were, in many respects, free to take charge of assembling their networks of friends from all sorts of sources.[4] In the later decades, however, some of the women did not choose to start making new friends. By this time they had established a small but stable network of friends and associates. They had pared back their friendships to a few "old reliables." Those who had become especially closely bonded with their spouses indicated that no one else could cross the perimeter of intimacy surrounding the married pair, and although they had no women friends, they felt no need to acquire them.

New Friends/No Friends

The faint stirrings that signaled the possible beginnings of a new friendship appeared to take place when the desire and the opportunity happened to coincide in the lives of two women. Although it might look at first glance as if the women had the freedom to pick and choose whomever they wanted for friends in a highly individualized fashion, there were actually a number of exterior and interior conditions of adulthood that put constraints on these free-lance endeavors. In the broadest terms, these constraints were both personal and social-structural in nature, some were limiting, while others were enabling. Just a few examples of these constraints must suffice at this point to suggest what has been developed more fully on the subject in later sections of the chapter. To illustrate the influence of personal constraints on friendship making, it should be noted that starting new friendships required the possession and mobilization of certain social skills that had to be subtly applied in each relationship. Some women seemed to have been early bloomers in these talents for friendship formation. Others had blossomed in mid or late season, or never. Shyness, for example, may have inhibited a woman from making friends in even the most salubrious environment.

In addition, some social settings discouraged the likelihood of making friends, regardless of the psychological attributes of the women who lived in them. There were women who had been good at making friends throughout adulthood but who later found themselves unable to acquire new friends when they had been transplanted to another part of the country. An outgoing woman in her sixties tried to account for her failure to make some new friends after she moved to the East Coast to live near her married daughter. She spoke in wistful tones:

> All my old friends are back in Indiana. We write some, send cards, and talk on the telephone, but we can't afford to do that too often. My closest friend back home—we went to graduate school together—is staying in Indianapolis, but other friends of hers and mine are moving away from the city to Florida, New Mexico, and so forth to retire, so she's no better off than I am. I am really stranded out here. There's no public transportation I can use, so I have to stay put until my daugher has time to take me somewhere.

Wanting friends, but not being able to make new friends, was not an unusual situation for a woman to find herself in at several distinct periods of her life. This occurred either when she had trouble reaching out to people or when she was not lodged in an ecological niche favoring the growth of friendship.

Although there were many ways that middle-class women went about starting new friendships, at the same time there were some commonalities in these beginnings that could be distinguished from the idiosyncrasies of any particular individual's friendship behavior. It was especially in the beginnings of the friendship relation that some discernible patterns emerged. What went on in the start-ups of their real-life friendships pointed to the enabling and constraining influence operating at the outset of a new relationship. Some of these patterns were recognizable in the excerpts from the friendship interviews that have been quoted and analyzed in the following sections. Who would become friends with whom? How long would it take to make some durable connections? How had women managed to get others to like them and want to be their friends? How many friends could they expect to make and keep?

IN THE BEGINNING

Although all the friendships of the women in the study had histories consisting of beginnings, middles, and, sometimes, endings, it was not always easy for a woman to put her finger on just how a particular relationship had been launched. It was difficult for her to say precisely what had made it progress through the early steps of the first introductions and casual acquaintanceship to that critical crossover point when she had first sensed that there was some degree of real attachment between the two of them and a feeling of permanence about the tie—some notion that it had a future. Even though every friend had a name, a personality, a setting, and a time of life in which the friendship took place, and every friendship experience was remembered as unique and was never confused with any other one, the memories of the transition from prefriendship to early friendship were fuzzy in most instances (the exceptions to this were notable). "It just happened," was a frequent comment. Others said, "I'm not exactly sure when we began thinking of each other as friends. We probably didn't even feel that way at the same time." And in greater detail: "It took a long, long time, many years of being together in the same office, then being separated when Amy took a job in another city. I know I wanted her to be my friend before she herself probably thought about it very much. I'd have a hard time identifying that passage from one stage of the relationship to the other. I think it's too blurred to say."

The Forgotten Preliminaries

For the most part, the women had not remembered taking mental notes on the formation of the friendship. It was also possible that they had forgotten most of what they had taken note of at the time. In their retrospective accounts of the process, some could specify a number of things they had done that were intended to cultivate the growth of an incipient friendship. "Sure, I called her after our first introductions to go some place I thought she'd enjoy. You often say you'll do this and don't follow up. But in her case I did." A vivacious young businesswoman said, "I always talked to her for a long time when I had the chance at a party instead of just hopping around like I usually do." An older woman explained that a much younger person was the one who took the initiative by suggesting that "we get together somewhere. I wasn't expecting to hear from her and I had really forgotten about her. But when she called and suggested we go out and do something, probably to see a movie, I was glad to go. I really felt flattered." Some recalled having hopes, which they scarcely admitted to themselves, that some of their exploratory moves at the beginning of an acquaintanceship might end in friendship. They mentioned disappointments and setbacks and real doubts about whether the relationship would ever gel. Even so, in the face of all these attempts to engage another woman in a friendship and in the cases where it took many years to develop the relationship, the women could seldom pinpoint the time at which their efforts had begun to bear fruit.

In the majority of cases, in fact, the women did not like to think of themselves as engaging in conscious strategies so clearly designed to create positive feelings in another person toward themselves. "I think that's demeaning our relationship," objected a fifty-year-old personnel officer. "It sounds so Machiavellian. I don't think it's a very good idea to analyze human relations that way. It kills the spontaneity." Instead they usually portrayed themselves as just taking part in the experience and enjoying it as it unfolded in the course of time. They conceived of themselves as not planning or even cultivating the growth of a relationship—much less maneuvering to forward its development. "I don't like to think of our friendship in that crass way," was the reply of a successful real estate broker. "It spoils it for me." In contrast, there were a number of women who were frankly pragmatic about devising strategies for winning friends. Although they recalled the gamut of emotions from pleasure and excitement to disappointment and resentment during early stages of the chase, they thought that their pursuit of friendship was in keeping with the style in which they did almost everything about which they were serious: they set goals, made plans for achieving them, and carried out activities designed to accomplish the objectives.

A few friends, but not many, had made a practice of having discussions about the positive and negative aspects of their tie to each other, including the preliminary phases of their relationship. Some of the sketchy data about these explorations have been included in the chapter on the extraordinary relationship between some best friends. In the main, however, the women who were friends did not sit around and talk about what went on in their own relationship. Instead of probing the nature of their own friendship, they had conversations about the events in the lives of the other people they knew. They analyzed situations and told stories about happenings that might have had parallels with the experiences of their own friendship over the years. During their second and third interviews some of the respondents came with fresh ideas about their friendships and discussed elements in the beginnings of their relationships that they had taken the time to dig out of their memories. They had been interested in figuring out how the early stages of an important friendship might have set the stage for the later interaction between the pair. It was a rich field to explore by the pairs of friends themselves.

Memories: Good, Bad, and Indifferent

Current estimates by friends of the quality of a friendship made a critical difference in the nature of the retrospective account of its origins. If the relationship had developed into a close, long-term friendship, the beginnings were likely to be highly romanticized. There was delight in telling stories about the "silly things we did." But these "silly things" and other more serious events had ordinarily not been understood as being significant at the time they happened. Besides there had been a whole series of such experiences in a developing friendship, not just one or two particularly memorable ones. The incremental moves toward each other were not only numerous, but also infinitesimally small, and many of these had not been steps toward each other, but side steps, back steps, and steps taking the women away from the relationship, if only temporarily, while other people—husbands, lovers, parents, children, and other friends—had dominated their attention and caused them to neglect a developing friendship. To sum up, there had not been a straight road of development and, to change the metaphor, there had been no recognizable single moment of flowering that had announced the existence of a friendship.

If, on the other hand, a friendship had bloomed and then faded, the trouble taken to get the friendship started was almost always remembered as a bad investment. The loss had consisted of all the time and energy taken from other activities and other friendships. But the greater losses were the emotional ones: they were remembered as feelings of disillusionment and a good deal of pain that they had suffered during and after the breakup of a close friendship. Women seldom volunteered information about failed relationships. The subject was not considered for discussion and then discarded on the assumption that the topic of lost friends should not be included in an account of their friendships. It simply did not occur to them to talk about the decline and death of a friendship. More about the dissolution of relationships and disengagements of friendship pairs will be discussed in the subsequent chapters devoted to the processes of cultivation and repair of friendships and their breakdowns and endings.

In other kinds of friendships, such as the run-of-the-mill, more ordinary types, the first places and times of meeting were easily recalled, as was the case in all the friendships of any duration, but the transition from acquaintanceship to friendship was regarded as uneventful and uninteresting to explore. Because a great many women included "my ordinary, pretty good friends" in their catalog of friendships and, as a thirty-three-year-old mother at home with two babies said, "my friend of convenience is a very valuable friend," it was evident that ordinary friends, possibly second tier in rank of closeness, could not possibly be excluded as an important type of friend. Rather, they should be counted in for what they were: relationships giving specific benefits—probably of different sorts to each friend. Friendships of convenience provided both women with things they wanted, often in less global ways than closer friends, but were nevertheless pleasurable and appreciated by both women. In fact, many women put all their friends in this general category, although they did not label the relationships as run-of-the-mill or ordinary just because they were limited. What they said was, "I go to museums with Frances." Or, "I'm crazy about Cindy's kids and like to go places with the three of them." "I like all my friends for different reasons. Nobody has everything I want in one person." And to characterize such friendships more fully: "If you are trying to discover when I felt we were really beginning to feel like friends, it was *not* when I felt we were more intimate or close or something like that. That's not what I mean by friendship. I don't need that, but I know I have a great bunch of friends" (Hess, 1972).

Initial Reactions

By Betsy's account, her friendship with Velma had not started off with a bang. The initial contacts between them had been anything but dramatic. In fact, they had scarcely given each other a second thought after the first glimpse of each other at the time Betsy and her family had moved into the enclave of large houses where Velma had lived for a good twenty years. There had been no evidence of particularly "good chemistry" or "clicking from the start" to let them know intuitively about the existence of some natural affinity between them. Although a few of the friendships between the adult women in the study had been announced with sirens and flashing lights, most had started off gradually, just as Velma and Betsy's had done.

Concerning her initial reaction to Velma, Betsy reported that she could not remember it distinctly, but she thought she had liked her about equally as much as the other women she happened to meet at the time she was busy settling into her new house and preparing the courses she was teaching at the university. Thinking of the time before she and Velma had become such good friends, Betsy tried to recapture what was on her mind then:

I don't know. I certainly didn't *dislike* her. I guess I'd have to say I was sort of neutral about all the women I met those first months. I was just trying to find a convenient supermarket, a pediatrician, a dentist, a bank, all that stuff you have to put in place quickly. I was backing up Dan, too, and, of course, the three girls, trying to make everything go smoothly at their new school and I had to attend all those formal receptions and dinners connected with Dan's new job.

Just as with Betsy's response to Velma, most of the women said that they seldom knew at the outset that they would eventually become good friends with another woman. They might have sensed the possibilities for friendship early on, but, they said, it would have been foolhardy to forecast the growth of a friendship on such slim evidence. Contrary to what a large body of research findings about interpersonal attraction would lead us to expect—that an instant response to others (usually by college students in a laboratory) indicated a preference for one individual over another—in real life the women had not recognized a potential bosom friend at first sight. There was no way to predict the development of the complex relationship involved in a friendship on the basis of something as simple as initial attraction.

Between some first attraction, if indeed that had occurred, and the beginnings of even a preliminary acquaintanceship, all kinds of trial-and-error moves were made. Some of these were inner calculations: "I'm never confident about whether or not the other person was as attracted to me as I was to them when we were first introduced," an older woman who was a mental health professional admitted. "I know I hold back. I guess I don't appear to be timid. No one would call me that at the place I work, but I actually feel unsure about people's initial reaction to me." Feeling this way, this woman and many others frequently failed to follow up good prospects among the men and women to whom they said they had positive reactions, people with whom they felt they would be compatible and whom they would be interested in getting to know better. But for a variety of reasons—lack of time, scheduling conflicts, and simple failure to take the trouble to make the arrangements for a meeting, as well as the timidity and shyness referred to—the women allowed many promising candidates to get away.

THE POOL OF ELIGIBLES

"Not disliking" Velma was a crucial judgment for the future of the friendship between Betsy and Velma, since this meant that Velma had not been eliminated at the outset from Betsy's pool of eligibles for selection as a friend. "We like to think," wrote psychologist Derek Wright, "that, though we may not be able to choose our neighbors, or the people we work with, nor our relatives, at least we can choose our friends" (Wright 1970). Realistically, however, for the women in the study, there were some conditions beyond their control that put real limitations on this so-called freedom of choice. Broadly speaking, their selections were exercised within the narrow bounds of the contacts they made with other women during their everyday comings and goings, and much more significant, their choices were subject to self-restrictions. The latter consisted of each woman's personal definitions of suitable candidates for friendship and of her judgments about whether these individuals would in turn be receptive to the prospects of becoming a friend of hers. All these attitudes and judgments were pretty well formed by the time the women had reached adulthood.

The women's friends had been acquired (we have found that choice and selection were misleading terms for the way women actually *became* friends) from pools of eligibles that varied in size from small birdbaths to oceans. The number of people they had the chance to meet varied so widely that it was difficult to grasp the sources of the commonalities of their friendship experience that obviously existed. For example, a businesswoman who traveled met hundreds of new people every year, whereas a woman at home with young children had almost no new contacts during the previous year. Yet they each had three good friends and a number of casual ones.

It was found that four concepts were needed to make some

headway in understanding the process of making and keeping friends: the women made use of their personal (1) dislike criteria, (2) disregard criteria, (3) liking criteria, and (4) their highly individual budgets of friendship as procedures for narrowing down a large unwieldy cast of candidates for closer relationships. "Friendship choices are made from a set of eligibles on the basis of 'liking criteria' "(Rodin 1982, 31). But first of all, the women eliminated people from this set of eligibles by means of two exclusion judgments. Everyone got rid of a miscellaneous assortment of potential friendship candidates by using their *dislike* and *disregard* criteria. Once individuals had met these initial exclusion criteria, no more attention was paid to them as friendship prospects.[5] Among those who survived the first round of cuts, friends were made by using *liking* criteria as a basis for considering the possibility of a relationship. However, of those who were left in the pool of eligibles after the cuts made by the *dislike* and *disregard* criteria, there could be so many remaining who were suitable friendship partners that something stepped in to limit the average number of friends of most of the women. This was called by us a personal *budget of friendship*, which operated to keep the average number of good friends to between two and five women.[6] Some women, however, could not resist the allure of the many attractive candidates and went on acquiring all comers. For example, one woman declared, "I have ninety personal friends we invited to my son's wedding." In contrast, the budgets of friendship for some women were filled by only one other person, who might be a woman, a man, or a child. The connections between the number of friends each woman had and the finite amounts of any woman's time and emotional energy have been dealt with in more detail later in the chapter (Shulman, 1975).

Disliking

The women had no trouble stating their grounds for rejecting certain people from the pool of eligibles from which they had already drawn their friends and would draw them in the future. One woman said, "I could never be friends with a political conservative," while another declared, "I just can't abide the dedicated activist type—for peace, women's causes, or such." "My pet peeve is a sloppy appearance," was Clara's version of a frequently expressed dislike judgment. Another woman said it this way: "I can't bear to be around grungy people. I can't understand why anyone would come to the office without showering." Another general category of disliking revealed class distinctions: "I realize this may sound snobbish, but ungrammatical speech grates on my nerves so much that I could never associate with anyone with that kind of background." By the tone of voice used to express how they rejected people with the disliked characteristics, there was no mistaking that such people were beyond the pale as far as further contact with them was concerned. Such people never managed to get past the first cut no matter what other endearing traits they might exhibit on further acquaintance.

"We never like people who meet our dislike criteria," Rodin observed, "regardless of what likeable qualities they may also possess" (Rodin 1982, 33). But under certain conditions the women modified some of their spontaneous dislike judgments that they ordinarily used to preclude getting to know others. Sometimes it happened that women were forced by circumstances to have regular contacts with disliked people. Neighbors and coworkers, for example, who had taken an immediate dislike to each other had, in some cases, gradually learned to appreciate each other's qualities enough to allow them to conduct friendly relations. One woman remarked about a neighbor, "We've come to an understanding that we won't discuss politics. I frequently have to bite my tongue when she says things she doesn't realize I can't bear to hear anyone say. I don't think she knows it, but her social and political attitudes keep me from considering her as a good friend as I would if she were not so conservative."

It also turned out that the woman who said she could not bear to be with sloppy women contradicted herself as she walked past a dowdy, rather disheveled woman on Nassau Street in Princeton. "There's somebody who would be fascinating to know. She might even be Albert Einstein's wife. Well, she's probably dead, but somebody who's her equivalent. But, you know, the town-gown separation in Princeton. You never have a chance to meet the university people no matter how much money you have." Physical unattractiveness was important in one context, but not in another. It became clear that the women held contradictory criteria for friendship in the same manner as they held incompatible beliefs about a host of other matters. They had no trouble living with the discordant attitudes about what they disliked in other people (Rokeach 1960).

The terminology in the English language to express disliking and liking proved to be so impoverished that it was difficult for the women to make the fine distinctions needed for their judgments about friends and nonfriends. This made it especially exasperating when trying to make distinctions between those women whom they left in the pool of eligibles (sometimes a large number) and those who ended up as their friends. The expression that was used by Betsy to describe how she first reacted to Velma was resorted to by many of the women. "Well, I didn't think we'd ever end up being friends. But I didn't *dislike* her." In addition, almost every one of their friends had characteristics that they did not like or actually disapproved of, and in many cases they knew of these disliked traits before their relationships had advanced to the point of friendship, or they discovered them later in the relationship. But these weaknesses and imperfections in those who were their friends did not end their friendships. In the course of almost every friendship the women had observed many unappealing attributes of their friends' attitudes, habits, and behavior, all possibly not only irritating and annoying, but also morally unacceptable. When these were discovered in a friend, they were usually excused and almost always laughed about. "Well, I have my faults too." Or, "Peggy's peccadilloes just go to prove that she's human after all. Otherwise, she'd be unbearable to live with." The excuses made for the various weaknesses and indiscretions of their friends signified that such characteristics had not touched any dislike criteria that could not be tolerated. Dislike judgments that were applied to a friend's behavior, such as lying and criticizing them or their families behind their backs, however, had ended some relationships.

In a later chapter some cases have been presented in which women dissolved established relationships when they found a friend's behavior unforgivable. They also broke up with friends when they heard negative reports, sometimes unfounded gossip, about them. At one time such friends had been very much liked but eventually had become very much disliked. At the same time there were friends who did things that created disturbing emotions, such as jealousy, guilt, disgust, and resentment over perceived neglect, yet the pair had managed not to break up. Strains and troubles between very good friends were not infrequent, yet these distressing aspects of friendship had not stopped the flow of liking, as evidenced by the survival of the relationship. Liking and a tolerated level of disliking were twin emotions that were almost never absent from friendships of any significantly deep level of importance to the pair. But there was also a fragility in the friendship bond that caused not-so-close friends and intimate friends to walk away from a friendship when some grounds for disliking was sufficiently strong. It appeared that the women had to deal with their dislike judgments throughout the life of any friendship. A commitment to a friend was tested all along the way by these judgments as well as by a woman's assessment of their significance to her for continuing a relationship.

Disregarding

The other way of excluding people from a pool of eligibles for friendship—which might have come either before or at the same time of applying personal dislike criteria—was by simply *disregarding* certain people. "Disregard cues," wrote Rodin, "function as unsuitability markers. They signify that the person will not meet our liking criteria, thus letting us 'know' at once that the person would not suit us as a friend. We do not dislike the people we disregard. . . . We . . . simply fail to notice them further" (Rodin 1982, 35). Although women realized when they themselves were being disregarded, they were not so conscious of their own disregarding behavior. The woman quoted earlier had been disregarded and expressed her discomfort when she said, "They just look right through you without batting an eye. I feel as though I'm invisible."

But disregarding took other forms than simply "looking right through you" and not speaking to everybody as they would to friends. It was engaged in by everyone on many occasions, since it would be impossible to treat the entire flow of traffic on a city sidewalk, for example, as if the people were on a first-name basis. It came into play in many social situations where people were guests or hostesses in "polite" company, such as at occasions of business and professional entertainment. Although the majority of the people attending such functions typically had the social background characteristics, financial standing, educational level, cultural interests, and other traits making them eminently appropriate as friendship partners for each other, the women dealt with the people at such gatherings as players in a ritualistic drama, not as unique individuals (Goffman 1955). They participated in official entertainment according to formal rules. Although people talked and laughed and acted as though they were being friendly, they actually were playing at engaging in personal interaction with the other guests. While they were fulfilling their roles as good guests, they had to be careful not to linger overly long with any single individual. At a reception attended by a sizable group of upper-middle-class people, the folkways required that the guests would make an effort to "mix" with the other guests. On these formal occasions their main aim was to meet their obligations and leave.

For some women who were either unaccustomed to the ritual or personally unable to bring off the act, being disregarded as a person and treating others as nonpersons were intensely uncomfortable roles to play (Goffman 1955, 1967). Others handled it easily, as explained by a society matron:

> We run in and out of these affairs as quickly as possible. In Washington, they don't expect you to stay long. We can do a wedding reception in twenty minutes. You're not trying to have real conversations. Boy, when one of those serious conversations starts up, my eyes glaze over. You have a drink, you go through the reception line, and you're out. You'll know some of the people, but that's not the point. Yes, I suppose you might already be friends with any number of them. Most of them you have run into very often, but you know these are formal receptions. They're not meant for anything more than that. It's not the place to strike up new acquaintances.

While at this sort of gathering, this woman had lumped all the other people together and taken them out of her pool of eligibles for new friends by one grand gesture of disregarding them as individuals, women also used their personal criteria for disregarding people in less wholesale ways. Although there were wide differences in the ways they responded to others as belonging to categories of people whom they would automatically ignore, in general they tended to disregard others on the basis of being dissimilar from themselves on certain counts. There were common and readily recognizable guideposts for disregarding others as prospects for further acquaintanceship. These dissimilarities almost always functioned as "Keep off the Grass" signs. As a general rule, they consisted of differences in race, educational attainment or cultural background, social position, economic status, intelligence, age, and mode of dress and grooming.

It might be supposed that a woman would modify her disregard criteria in order to make a few friends, particularly when she found herself in a new place and feeling lonely. But it took a prolonged period of desperate loneliness to cause that to happen, and it had rarely taken place among the women in the study. The case of a young professor illustrated how tenaciously disregard criteria were clung to even when, by her own account, she recognized that there had been at least some possibly suitable friendship candidates that she seemed to have dismissed summarily.

Carole had arrived on an Ivy League campus in the early 1970s. Armed with a brand new Ph.D. from a Big Ten university, she was the first woman appointed to a position in the political science department of all-male colleagues. She was a "gender pioneer" (Kanter and Stein 1979). As she put it quite bluntly, "when I came here I found the most distressing situation. There weren't any women. I mean literally there weren't any women. People would say to me, 'Oh Carole, I have a nice man to introduce you to,' and I would reply, 'Fine, does he have a sister? I need friends. I don't have any friends.' I was very unhappy." In Carole's mind she was making a factual statement when she said, "There weren't any women." Of course this judgment was arrived at by using her own disregard criteria. She added, without thinking, that what she said might have sounded a bit strange. "It is true," she admitted, "that I did meet women who were administrators and technicians and nonfaculty, but for the first four years—certainly, for the first three—I didn't have even one close woman friend. I can still remember the pain and desperation of not having any women friends." Her assumptions about the noneligibility of any woman who was not a faculty member wre implicit and unexamined. Her grounds for disregarding others as candidates for friendship were simply taken for granted. Instead she stuck to her friends living at a distance. "I used to spend a lot of time telephoning old friends," she explained, "and my airline bills were pretty high. It was a lonely time."

Even in her intense unhappiness over not having some women friends, Carole had never tried exploring the potential for establishing friendships with the many women around her ("the administrators and technicians and nonfaculty") to alleviate her emotional distress. Asked about this, she replied that she eventually had discovered many years later that the departmental secretary had political values that were more compatible with her own than almost anyone else on campus, and although the two of them grew to be on close terms and took part in some anti-rape demonstrations on campus for which it was not easy to recruit women as participants, still they had never become personal friends outside the office:

> The people I'm extremely friendly with now came here in my fourth year. They are women in other departments who got their jobs later and some are my graduate students, the older ones who are roughly my own age. There were some women here before me, some older women appointed maybe as early as the late 1950s, but, I don't know, they were never very cordial at the beginning and besides I don't think we would have gotten along especially well.

The disregard criteria Carole used and put high in her rankings were for people who were not her own age and not engaged in intellectual, scholarly pursuits similar to her own.

Age difference was a widely used disregard criterion.[7] There were a number of accounts of how strongly it operated, particularly among the younger women, as it applied to women who were as few as five years older than they were. For some of the thirty-year-olds, being thirty-five put another person into the category of middle-aged or "older woman" and beyond their cut-off point for "natural association." In fact, ageisms were a noticeable part of the disregard vocabulary of the younger women. "We're the first ones to move into a neighborhood of older couples. It's turning over, we hope. But until it does, we'll have to try to meet people elsewhere," said a new mother in her late thirties. "They put us at a table with a bunch of old codgers at the wedding dinner," complained another woman going on forty-five. "It was a terrible bore." On the other hand, some women said they had discovered that they enjoyed being with women of another age. A forty-year-old upwardly mobile draftswoman, for example, reported her surprise that she had found she liked

> a rich, old lady who was helping to stuff envelopes for the anti-nuke campaign. I always assumed they were all snobbish and wouldn't even speak to me when we were working together. It wasn't like that with her. We've become good friends. I go to her huge house and help her with her correspondence. She insists on paying me—and very well—and I can use the money. But that's not what matters. She's really a lovely person.

This younger woman's usual disregard and dislike criteria—those relating to age differences and her suspicions of the wealthy—had been breached by a positive personal experience that overruled her almost visceral rejection of the dissimilar, disliked, and disregarded. For her, it was a matter of "the we" against "the they" until she gave "the they" a chance to stay in the pool.

Most of the women were not conscious that they were being directed by these signs. They preferred to believe that something like race difference, for example, would not impose a kind of predetermined barrier to friendship. However, dissimilarities of these socially unacceptable kinds—and others that carried little social opprobrium—had mysterious powers. They triggered disregard behavior efficiently and lastingly unless and until a personal encounter with the ordinarily disregarded happened to occur and succeeded in challenging the judgment.

If asked whether they had ever considered making friends with a person whom they had automatically thought unsuitable on some general grounds, the women replied that they approached people as individuals—not as members of groups. They did not like being pigeonholed themselves, and they thought that age gaps, for example, were not impossible to cross and that race differences did not impose insurmountable barriers to friendship. They were reluctant to think that their personal relationships were shaped to any degree by some deterministic outside forces. They all knew that first impressions could be misleading. Most of these middle- and upper-middle-class women thought that they kept an open mind about people's qualities and would not reject them out of hand on account of some surface characteristics. As it turned out, though, the friends they actually had made, particularly those in the inner circle of close friends, almost always conformed to the dictates of their dislike and disregard criteria.

Liking

It was not exactly surprising, then, to find that the women in the sample had made friends of women and men who had roughly the same characteristics as themselves in respect to race, educational attainment, social position, economic status, intelligence, age, and even in mode of dress and grooming. This could be expected, since their *liking criteria* were, with some exceptions, the mirror images of their disregard judgments. Indeed similarities of many sorts, according to virtually the whole body of research findings on interpersonal attraction, were the main condition for liking another person (Newcomb 1961; Lazarsfeld and Merton 1954; Berscheid and Walster 1968). However, the brief encounters between strangers in a laboratory experiment or students in a dormitory had little resemblance to the actual experience of adults meeting for the first time during the ordinary course of living. Initial attraction also failed to predict whether the people who liked each other would pursue the relationship beyond the moment. In the laboratory research on attraction patterns, the subjects were never kept track of after they had left the testing rooms, so there were no findings to show how these immediate feelings of attraction would be acted on subsequently. In fact, the women in the study said that they had often met others whom they found attractive, yet simply had no wish to see again. Although the patterns of attraction and liking, which have been demonstrated in the laboratory, were not adequate explanations for the beginning of the enduring relationships that the women in the sample talked about, still some sort of liking was obviously an essential ingredient in the beginning of many friendships.

It should be emphasized once again that there were wide individual differences in what sparked an interest in another person sufficient to make them think about seeing a person again, and thus not abort the possibility of some future interaction. This was consonant with the demonstrated laboratory evidence that people liked others with attributes similar to their own and, the corollary to this, that the kinds of similarities that were associated with liking seemed to be virtually endless in number. In fact, there were so many that only a few of them can be mentioned. The main categories of attraction consisted of similarities of interests, attitudes, and values (Byrne 1971); equivalent socioeconomic means and status (Hartup, Glazer, and Charlesworth 1967); being approximately the same age (Verbrugge 1977); and many others. The studies showed that people liked individuals whose personalities were similar to their own (Duck 1973, 1977a, 1977b). People also responded positively to others whom they perceived as liking them by liking them back (Backman and Secord 1959). They regularly preferred physically attractive people over less attractive ones (Dion, Berscheid, and Walster 1972; Stroebe et al. 1971). They were usually friends with people of the same sex (Dickens and Perlman 1981).

Although the friendships of the women in the study always consisted of some degree of liking and invariably included a collection of some of these similarities (it would be hard not to share a number of them), such traits and behavior and background characteristics were never sufficient in themselves to explain the bonds between particular friends. Clearly this was because every woman had her own hierarchy of likes that she used after narrowing the field of eligibles by excluding most people early on by either disregarding them altogether or using dislike criteria to eliminate them as possible friendship partners.

Strong initial attraction did play a part in the beginnings of some friendships, but not in all of them. Although the women in the study regularly moved among people who were similar to themselves in a great variety of ways, not all the people they associated with were considered likable enough by them to qualify for friendship. Or, there were so many who qualified that it was impossible to befriend them all. As it turned out, their good friends not only met a number of their requirements for liking them, but they also were likely to frequent places and settings in which their relationship could be pursued conveniently and where they both enjoyed spending time. The greater the variety of the pleasurable occasions in which the friendship could develop, the stronger the likelihood that the women would eventually get to know each other better.

To sort out the few who had eventually become friendship pairs from all the others in the field of eligibles, it was occasionally quite easy to fasten on what had provided the impetus to get the relationship going. Some of the women had indelible memories of sensing the magnetism of another woman's personality. Dora, who was in her mid-fifties and the wife of a businessman, reminded herself of the reasons she was drawn so strongly to Jackie: "It's funny," she said, "that you can't remember how a friendship started, but with Jackie the special thing that I remember about the beginning was that she kept her front door open when she was home and you knew that meant she was there for her friends to drop in." Dora's response seemed almost physical to Jackie's warmth and open-door hospitality, which also had great appeal for a number of other women. "Jackie was a kind of focal point of our neighborhood," Dora explained. "If I was out shopping, on my way back I always stopped by. Sure enough, I would be there five or ten minutes, and in would walk Bea. Then someone else would come in, you know, and it was wonderful. You didn't have to call her and ask if you could come over. It was a great feeling to know she was always there and enjoyed having you drop in. She just loved it."

Dora was not a pushover for a show of friendliness that was just skin deep. She came to Jackie with city-bred suspicions that Jackie might be putting on an act. She shared the common difficulty of making accurate inferences from others' behavior and she needed to check out whether her availability was genuine or merely a surface veneer. This was a tricky assessment to make, particularly for middle-class women, who almost always treated their social equals courteously and, in some cases, with misleading cordiality. In fact, Dora remembered taking a "wait-and-see" stance toward Jackie to find out if Jackie really reciprocated her feelings of attraction. Dora told how skittish she had been:

You see, I'm a city person who didn't even know my next door neighbor, and here was a woman who was so open and warm and, besides that, charming and witty. But she wasn't just that. If you were down, she could make you laugh, and she also cried with you. All us city people loved it. You could drop in there all dressed up fit to kill or you could go in with an old robe thrown over your nightie. You didn't have to stand on ceremony.

Jackie was a kind of person whom Dora had never run across before. She possessed a number of personality traits that the research on personal attraction had documented as being surefire friendmakers, one of which was being outgoing. In general, most people, it was found, preferred extroverts to introverts (Hendrick and Brown 1971). "It was the ease of the relationship that was so special," Dora went on to say in elaborating on both the initial attraction to Jackie and the confirming knowledge that Jackie was not just pretending to be friendly when they met at a social gathering. "It wasn't long after I met her at a party that I was drawn to her and began dropping by every time I was out on an errand." Not only had Jackie not proved to be disappointing on further acquaintance, but she had indicated by the way she welcomed Dora that she returned her feelings of attraction and regard. What Dora had observed, however, was that the three women who felt so attracted to Jackie had not developed a similar relationship with one another. "It's strange," said Dora, "but the three of us who were closest to her couldn't act that way with each other."

If friendship were predictable merely on the basis of matching up women with similar backgrounds, this information about the similarities of these women (who were close friends of Jackie but not of one another) would not be sufficient to predict the development of friendship. Frequently women did not establish friendships with the friends of a close friend, even though they were introduced and thrown together on many occasions. There were so many elements in the complex relationships that the ultimate mix in a single friendship was unique to each one.

In the accounts of initial attraction—and it must be mentioned again that strong attraction did not always typify the beginnings of friendship—there were many commonalities in the behavior that had elicited immediate liking or at least interest in getting to know another person. Women were described as having ways of interacting with others that set them outside the routine of just being polite, acting friendly, and observing the social amenities. "She looked at me so intently that I felt she really cared about what I was saying," one woman recalled. Another explained her developing friendship with a man in his late thirties. "I found him just fascinating when he talked about his years in Nigeria in the Peace Corps." A middle-aged woman broke into a broad smile and said, "I knew I was going to like her when I first heard her laugh." A divorced woman in her forties explained what happened when a new professional was added to the staff: "It was not just attraction. I wouldn't use that word. There was something absolutely commanding about her to me. I felt impelled to get to know this person. What was it? It was her intellect."

The force of personality, style of interacting, intensity of interest in activities and ideas, all these were sources of special attraction. A few women called it "charisma." But there were quiet and unobtrusive manners that seemed equally compelling. One of the more frequently mentioned kinds of initial attraction was appearance and style of dress. Shirley explained what had attracted her to her close friend Lois before she even knew who she was: "I first noticed Lois, " Shirley said, "when I saw her shopping a couple of different times in my corner grocery store. She was always so well put together. It didn't matter whether it was Saturday and she was in pants or right after work in office clothes. She just stood out." Lois had not only caught Shirley's attention, but had also stimulated a positive response to her appearance a number of times. The positive response was significant because Shirley also paid attention and reported on women whose appearance she disapproved of and described with words like "slovenly," "dumpy," "housewifey," and "no taste in clothes," "a real dog." Shirley herself never left the house not looking presentable. In her descriptions of her friends, she always described their appearance in great detail, both praising and criticizing them for their clothing, hairstyles, and makeup.

Just as all the women had their individual reasons for their initial attraction and their early feelings of liking for the women who had eventually become their friends, Shirley used her own yardstick for making an initial judgment about whether she could find someone compatible. Using appearance as one of her criteria allowed her to include Lois in her set of eligibles for friendship even before they had been introduced. Physical attractiveness, good grooming, and fashionable attire were her particular *sine qua non* for an individual to qualify as her possible social companion. Of course the fact that Lois had passed the qualifying test would not necessarily convert into liking and befriending her.

But women often used an expression like "I really liked her from the start" and then went on to specify one of a variety of traits of their current friends, positive feelings that had prompted them to follow up on the relationship. Just as people regularly do, Shirley had used a hunch about certain outward appearance that told her other things about Lois. She had applied her own "implicit personality theory" to make an educated guess about other qualities Lois would have (Schneider, Hastorf, and Ellsworth 1979). These would tell her that Lois would probably have certain personality traits, interests, activities, educational level, possessions, tastes, and life style. Psychologists have found that people believe that there are a set of correlations among all these characteristics. "Pick one or see one and you can count on the rest pretty much falling in place," explained one canny member of the sample. That would have encouraged Shirley to believe, for example, that women who were fashionably dressed were likely to be what she hoped they would be: "fun to be with, interested in a lot of current things, not too stuffy or overserious about life, and ready to go places. It may sound superficial, but I find it usually works." Although these correlations had not always turned out to be accurate, most of the women seemed to rely on such cues about people from which they would infer some probable compatibilities between them, if they should ever become acquainted. As a result, it could happen that first impressions gave some indications that a relationship might be worth pursuing. Of course the cues and the correlations that were made by each individual came out of the diverse experiences of the women and reflected their unique life histories, their individual developmental patterns, and the social and intellectual climates in which they came to maturity.

So it could be said that there was a predictable "fit" of friends, one to another. But there were also a good many unpredictables. For example, by virtue of living together as assigned roommates in college, or in the course of living side by side as neighbors for many years, or from the daily interaction of working in the same office, surprising combinations of dissimilars—sometimes virtually opposites on a number of important variables—had gradually come to accept these differences and develop lasting relationships. In these friendships it appeared to be true that opposites were not attracted, but on becoming acquainted could and did learn to like each other and become friends.

THE BUDGET OF FRIENDSHIP

Depending on the age of the woman at the time she was interviewed, whether she was in her thirties, forties, fifties, or sixties, she had what we have called her own personal budget of friendship. This metaphor was used to convey the notion that there were on one side of this budget ledger available friendship resources and, on the other side, the network of friends that she had developed from these resources. The size and composition of her friendship network resulted both from her cultivation of the resources and from what appeared to be some natural limitations on the number of friends who could, on the average, be "managed" by any individual. There were practical limitations on the conceivable interactions between a woman and the people she knew.

As far as could be told from the interviews, the entries into both sides of an individual budget of friendship were influenced by five general conditions. First, there was the availability to each woman of a pool of eligibles for friendship made up of all the people she had met and could have made an effort to meet. It has already been pointed out that some settings provided a wealth of candidates for friendship, while others were stingy with supplies of suitable companions. Second, there were the people who had survived the automatic rejection stemming from her dislike and disregard judgments and then had met her liking judgments. Third, her budget of friendship was greatly affected by her individual need for sociability and intimacy, which is called the need for affiliation, or affiliation motivation, by social psychologists (McClelland 1953; Atkinson 1958; DeCharms and Moeller 1962). Both the level of sociability and the preference for privacy varied considerably among the women in the sample. Fourth, her budget of friendship was restricted by the finite amounts of time and emotional energy she possessed and devoted to all social relationships (Shulman 1975). Finally, the size and character of her budget of friendship were greatly affected by the social skills with which she picked out suitable candidates for friendship, then became further acquainted with these prospects, and, finally, by the effectiveness of the means she used to cultivate these friends over the long term. Each of these three latter aspects of making friends involved distinctly different personal skills (Cook 1977). In the end it appeared as if there were some natural forces operating to limit the first-tier friends to one or two persons, while second-tier friends numbered about four or five, and so on to larger numbers as involvement tapered off.

The composition and size of a friendship network, then, could be regarded as the consequence of the ways a woman had deployed her human resources for making friends. Her opportunities for friendship were greatly influenced by the personal and social circumstances in which her life was imbedded throughout adulthood. The general nature of the resulting social network—that is, the number and kinds of people, the intensity of the relationships, and the density of the connections among these associates and friends—changed and evolved in many directions over the years (Fischer 1977). Yet at every stage there appeared to be some limitations on the number of individuals with whom any one person could form friendships and keep as active relationships. In addition, the number of people designated as friends depended entirely on the individual's definition of friendship. Most of the women used complex hierarchies for ranking their friends, and they used intricately defined cut-off points between degrees of closeness to these people.

How Close/How Many

When trying to put their current friends in rank order of closeness, the women were certain about the placement of those closest to them, but others were harder to place—they seemed to cross back and forth between the boundaries of the second, third, and more distant tiers. "Let's see, now," said the interviewer in her schoolmarm voice, which she used when making summaries at the end of a classroom lecture. "How many friends would you say you have, right now? Why don't you try counting them up—by naming the ones you've just described." The answer to the question of how many friends a woman had was seldom straightforward, partly because of the difficulties and uncertainties involved in applying general notions about friendships to specific people. The question precipitated a second try at giving her definition of friendship, then ranking friends in degree of closeness, and, finally, reconsidering earlier decisions about which people fitted into which slots.

At this point it became clear that each woman's personal budget of friendship included both the realities of how many friends she had and her hopes and dreams for future relationships, including regrets over misspent and wasted resources, assessments of sound investment in present friendships, and some calculations on how to deploy available resources in the future. As with all personal budgets, there had been opportunities and constraints imposed by the realities of the individual's circumstances. A woman's perceptions of the ideal number of friends were affected by her past experience with friendship and her sense of how many relationships of the kind she defined as friendship were "manageable," given her commitment to other relationships and activities. Consequently a budget of friendship was both a wish list and an accounting of the realities of her life.

There was a distinct split in the women's views on the chances they had for making some new friends. A minority thought there were so many potential friends standing in the wings that they would, regrettably, never have the time and energy to bring them to center stage. Their budgets of friendship seemed to be bursting at the seams. For a large majority of the women, however, adulthood had involved a slackening off of prospects for making new friends. Their budgets of friendship seemed to be contracting. Once they had settled into a place of residence and begun rearing a family or working on their careers, they thought they had used up most of their chances to meet new people. "Once you've lived around somebody a long time or worked with them for a number of years and not found anything that clicked, you don't suddenly start being buddy-buddy with them," said a fifty-year old woman who had worked in a medium-sized manufacturing company for about a dozen years. "In the small office where I'm a supervisor," explained a forty-two-year-old woman whose social service agency had been decentralized to reach more clients, "we don't hire that many new people, so there aren't many fresh starts I can make." A common complaint of single heads of households was that they almost always rushed home after work to make dinner for the children, so they could not go out to socialize with the employees after work. Of course sometimes circumstances had changed and friends had been made. But for most of the women, finding people to befriend had not been an easy task.

In answer to the question about current friendships, while most of the women said they had some "very good, very close," or "some pretty good" friends, others had "really no one I would call a close friend, as I would define it and want it. No one who I could say really listens to me and what I have to say." A thirty-one-year-old publicist working at a New York City book publishing company said sadly, "I've been so disappointed in the women I thought were my friends. Just last year one of them canceled a lunch appointment at the last minute because of a man. She said she knew I'd understand, but I was very angry with her. The only person I find I can really count on is my husband." This woman did not think it would be worth trying to find some other, more reliable female friends. "I just think that's the way things are," was her comment.

Another set of women, however, who came from all the age-decades said they felt lonely and expressed a desire to make some new friends. They were still hoping to find at least one good friend. But most of the women did not think that the number and the nature of their friendships would change drastically after mid-adulthood. "I know my patterns of behavior pretty well by now," a clinical psychologist in her late forties said, "and I don't expect I'll alter them that much unless something drastic happens, like the sudden death of my husband or the loss of our business. Even so, I think my ways with social relationships are pretty well established by now. In a crisis, of course, you never know."

OPPORTUNITIES FOR FRIENDSHIP

The number of people considered by the women as potential partners in friendship and whose paths had crossed theirs during an individual lifetime seemed fairly limited for most of the women, although others seemed aware of a broader field of contacts that they might make.[8] Some women had made valiant attempts to broaden the scope of their eligibles so that they might end up with a greater variety to pick from, but as hard as they seemed to try, the likelihood of widening the array of suitable partners to befriend was minimal. Most people ended up drawing their friends from the small pool of people around whom they lived and worked and played. Proximity indeed was fate for the beginnings of new friendships. There was a kind of psychological space of available individuals—its boundaries set the universe in which people traveled side by side and occasionally stopped long enough to become acquainted. Moreover, there were periods in their lives in which particular circumstances militated against even giving much thought to taking some actions to begin new friendships.

Charlene had worked in Boston for seven years before she was married and moved to a small city where her husband had worked and lived for about ten years. "He knew a lot of people in the area. One of the things I said to him before we got married was that I hoped he would help me meet people and make new friends. As it turned out, I felt that I didn't get as much help from him as I would have liked. He's much more outgoing than I am, so I don't really think it was his fault that it took me so long to make friends. It was for a number of reasons."

The reasons for not finding new friends quickly were not uncommon for the average working woman: they centered around time limitations and competing responsibilities as well as certain personality characteristics, such as being introverted. Charlene explained:

> I was starting on a new job, I had just moved, I got married, I had left the job I was accustomed to, I had left my best friend back in Boston, and then almost a month to the day after we got married, my father died. There were a lot of adjustments I had to make during that period. I was trying to keep a watchful eye on my mother, going back and forth to be with her on weekends. I also found I had to bring work home at night from my new job, and meanwhile I was trying to fix up our townhouse. So I didn't have a lot of time to devote to making new friends, not to mention to try to make a new marriage work.

For this woman the supply of potential of friends was limited by her busy schedule of competing obligations. As a consequence, the people who happened to buy houses near hers were preselected for her by fate as friendship candidates. As she told it, the purchase of a house had "pretty much determined how my husband and I had eventually made a group of good friends." Charlene recalled how it had taken place:

> It was five years ago that we bought a house in the development. On the first Christmas one of the families we had known before we moved in had a party for the neighborhood so we could get to know everybody. But again, time was a factor, so we didn't pick up on that right away. At this point my husband was commuting to work by train to New York, so he left home at 7A.M. and didn't get back until 7P.M. Then last year we invited everyone to a party around Memorial Day. That kind of got us going, and ever since then we really made a group of good friends among the neighbors, finally, after I had been married for four years.

Although the sources of a woman's friends were usually confined to the places she had lived in the past and where she currently resided, sometimes she cherished the hope that a fresh supply of interesting and available candidates for friendship would turn up, even though she did not see much prospect for that happening. In answer to the question "Would you like to make a new friend?" the majority of the women of all ages answered positively to the general idea. They did not like to think that they were beyond making new beginnings and disliked very much thinking that they might never add to their present circle of friends. Some women seemed to hold onto the notion that a wonderful new friend might suddenly descend from nowhere to brighten their lives. This remained in the realm of the wish system, which was an aspect of the romanticized conception of perfect friendships clung to by some women. Most women were more realistic about what they could expect from every kind of human relationship.

The Fast Start

In a few instances unusual efforts were made to cast a wider net to catch new friends. Gabrielle, a vivacious, well-to-do woman in her early forties, for example, brought back friendship trophies from her worldwide travels. In fact, she appeared to be more successful at starting up new friendships in places away from home base than in continuing her old friendships at home.

> Our meeting Megan and Christopher on the Costa del Sol was just heaven-sent. Here we were—my husband, Howard, and I—on our winter vacation, rapidly getting bored to death with each other's company. Time was already hanging heavy on my hands after a few days, even though the skies were always cloudless and I had started to get a good tan. We were at a little leather shop in town when we started chatting with a couple we recognized from our hotel. They were from London and seemed very nice.

Gabrielle acted on her hunch that they might be a compatible couple: "So when we came down for dinner that same evening, we joined them at their table with their two boys. We got off to a really good start. Howard noticed that Megan was reading Golding's book that had just been published and we had brought a copy along to read too. So it worked out that we had all kinds of things in common, like books, films, and politics."

At the outset Gabrielle had been looking only for some temporary companionship. "It just seemed natural that we would be together part of the day in the sun, have drinks and dinner, but we had this extra bonus of getting to know their two boys, whom we learned to adore. Ian was the serious student. Cory was more of a cut-up, an adorable kid. Howard agreed to extend our reservations to coincide with their holiday and we stopped off in London to visit them on the way home." It was the women who pursued the relationship beyond the usual short duration of friendships made while on vacation: "We've had this steady correspondence ever since between Megan and me, not the men, and visits back and forth between Toronto and London."

Leisure and affluence put couples like this in the enviable position of increasing the sheer number of people from whom they could draw their friends. But their friendship budget also drew a line on how many close friends they could realistically maintain. "About making friends overseas," Gabrielle commented,

> once we started being involved with Meg and Chris, we allowed a friendship we made with a lovely American couple we met in Acapulco

to lapse. We found ourselves being torn between spending time with the two couples when we made our holiday plans. I think that essentially the attractions were greater between us and the Ladds, and besides, Howard could combine some business in London with seeing them, which wasn't the case when we visited the American couple in Seattle. But we did keep on exchanging Christmas cards with the American couple we no longer saw regularly.

The fast starts at friendship at poolside in Acapulco seemed to be different from those made at the park with other mothers of young children and at the office with colleagues. The difference was more in the pace than in the process of getting started on an acquaintanceship. Friendships struck up at resort hotels—somewhat like shipboard romances—did not pause for decent intervals of separation and mellowing. They burned quickly and brightly, and their chances for survival were slim. But some of them lasted by virtue of the women taking the time to keep in touch through letters and reunions that were painstakingly planned and carried out to assure the continuation of the relationship.

The Slow Start

Most of the moves in the direction of friendship were almost imperceptibly slow. Perhaps it was a kind of wisdom in personal relations that recognized the need for an incubation period of some months, frequently a year or more. Although the infant relationship would not grow if completely neglected, it seemed to thrive on rather measured attention. It grew better without overfeeding, without pushing its development. If the flower of friendship was forced with exaggerated expectations, it was likely to fade quickly. Unlike adolescent friendships, those that were undertaken by adult women usually matured slowly and almost always carried much less emotional intensity. Instead of wooing each other in a frantic desire for response, women acquired their friends at a slow pace in the course of their daily routines at home or in the office, or while engaging in some recreational or organizational activity. "Friendship is less impetuous than a romantic relationship: it takes a much longer time to form than a romantic one," one of the women observed.

The various studies of the acquaintanceship process have come to the conclusion that it is typical for friendship to develop gradually (Kurth 1970). It is generally agreed that "the growth of relationships and the increase of intimacy have a tentative, propositional and experimental quality, with partners often making their 'moves' ambiguously in order to protect themselves against the consequences of their partner's refusal to accept growth which also (and therefore) can be done subtly and without affront" (Duck 1981c, 8). This early testing, as described by the women, took the form of tentative gestures, such as "Could you come over for coffee?" "How about lunch?" or "Why don't you stop by for a drink?" The responses to such approaches were carefully watched. The subjects of the friendships study almost never spoke of the equivalent of "falling in love," but more in terms of "coming to love" (respect, have affection for, enjoying) a friend.

In the case of Betsy and Velma, who lived three houses from each other in an area of spacious houses and three-acre lots, it had taken a year beyond the perfunctory nods and telephone calls to begin something. Their situations in regard to friends were at opposite poles. Velma, on the one had, was a longtime resident of the suburb and had become friends with two neighbors as well as with several other women at the hospital where she did volunteer work. At age forty-eight she was well settled into her family life and social arrangements with others, certainly not in need of including another woman in her busy schedule. Her budget of friendship was filled up. In contrast, Betsy was a newcomer who had recently parted in tears from dear friends halfway across the country. She was painfully aware that she had to make an effort to replace them, not knowing how long it would take and whether she would succeed in breaking into any of the pairs already established in the new location. "I know I have to have somebody to talk to. I need at least one good friend," Betsy said. Luckily for her, the eldest of her three daughters was the same age as Velma's youngest. It was a typical instance of children paving the way for frequent contacts between their mothers. Betsy described the slow pace of the development of her friendship with Velma:

It was the early summer when we arrived here, so Velma's youngest was away at camp as usual. After she returned in August and school started, she and my Sue rode on the bus to the Quaker School together and got to playing Monopoly to fill the time during the trip. That was the way the two of them got to know each other and they became fast friends, the way twelve-year-olds do, you know, always at each other's house, staying for meals, spending the night, and so forth.

This meant that Betsy and Velma had to talk to each other to make the arrangements for their children. Betsy explained that this started out on an impersonal basis: "So Velma and I were on the phone checking out where the kids were, giving the okays to stay over. But it wasn't until the next spring that Velma and I began talking a lot about other things and doing things together. She doesn't go crazy forcing herself on anybody." Meanwhile, over that first winter, Betsy had managed to make a friend of another neighbor, to whom she felt closest until her friendship with Velma took precedence:

My other friend here is Patty. She is the mother of the friend of my second child, Kim, and we got to know each other through the kids too. But she doesn't call me to do things a lot like Velma does. Patty's a friend and very close, but she's not like Velma. She's much nearer to my own age, but she's next best. Velma is first. There's something about me. I always get closest to someone quite a bit older than me.

With these two friends and another whom she had met through her part-time teaching job at a local university, Betsy felt satisfied. In fact, it was about all she could handle. Now her budget of friendship was filled.

My third daughter, the youngest, has a friend who has just moved into this neighborhood. Poor little Christine, she is kind of hurt because she keeps saying, "Mommy, when are you going to do something with *my* friend's mother? Why don't you go pick up Mrs. Moore?" But, you know, I guess you get a little selfish. You don't put yourself out so much after awhile because you're comfortable with the friends you have.

Who was left to befriend the mother of "poor little Christine's" friend when she arrived in a new neighborhood in which everyone was already taken? We never had a chance to hear her story, but if she followed the same path taken by most women, she was compelled to hunt for friends elsewhere or suffer from loneliness. Being suddenly stranded without companionship in a totally unfamiliar environment was an experience faced at some time—and often repeatedly—by women who changed residences so frequently. They were not necessarily prepared for starting the acquaintance process all over again. Several years after the interview Betsy had to leave the three friends she had made and start all over again, when the family moved back to the Midwest. This time it was not so difficult, since she and her husband had kept in touch with old friends, and there were some members of the family living nearby.

Friendship-Starting Skills

Sometimes it took a special event that allowed women who had known each other a long time without becoming friends to see each other in a new light—one that would allow them to consider moving beyond formal roles to a more personal relationship. This was true in the case of Shirley and Anita, who were both members of a real estate firm. They had known each other at work for ten years, and during that time, as Shirley put it, "we were like dogs sniffing each other." Shirley talked about the way they both approached their jobs. "I am driven. I am very, very success oriented in my work. To me, success means money, underlined. It's that simple. If you can imagine it, Anita is even more driven than I am." Over the years there had been a number of times when Shirley felt that Anita was trying to take advantage of her. Her anger at being treated so shoddily by Anita came out into the open after Shirley had spent time showing houses and making a sale to one of Anita's customers while Anita was on vacation for a month.

> When she returned from the Cape, she offered me one hundred dollars for doing all the work on the sale of a one hundred twenty-five thousand-dollar home. All she had left to do was to go to the closing and collect the money. So I said to her, "Do me a favor, Anita. In the future I won't do for you and you won't do for me." After that it was never mentioned again. She was always very courteous, very pleasant. I was the same with her.

Then something happened to break the ice between them:

About two years ago I was on the phone at the office. It was a Sunday and every button on the line was lit. A call came in for Anita and I didn't take the fellow's telephone number. When I called her to tell her he had called, she said to me, "You didn't get the number because it was for me. For somebody else you would have gotten the number." I said, "Anita, you're crazy. Every light was lit. There was no way I could handle all the calls by myself." So she comes roaring into the office, and she's going through the customer book, where you are supposed to put down every customer and their telephone numbers—lots of times we forget—and I see she's looking to see whether I put down the numbers for the other girls' customers.

At this juncture it was Shirley who decided to break the mold into which their relationship had formed during the eight years they had worked together. She and Anita have talked about what they would have missed if she had not made the move. "I say to her," Shirley recalled, " 'Anita, sit down. Really, you know, this is ridiculous. It's pouring cats and dogs and there is no way we are going to be showing houses. Just stop and think about the things you're saying to me and I'm saying to you.' And we both started to laugh." That episode marked the beginning of their new relationship. "Now," Shirley continued, "we have an extremely close friendship. It all seems very funny now, the way we used to act."

Overtures: Start and Stop

Who was available at a particular time and place played an important part in the initial pairing of acquaintances. However, some of the promising prospects for turning mere acquaintances to friends did not work out. Because many beginnings failed to develop beyond the initial stage of a relationship, they were quickly forgotten and, consequently, not included in most friendship histories. In some cases, however, hopes for them were not given up entirely on the chance that they might blossom later. Geraldine, a supervisor of counselors in a social service agency, spotted a woman she hoped to make into a friend, a social worker named Alice.

[redacted]

Her closest friend, Jane, lived too far away to see or talk with on a daily basis: "When my best friend, Jane, and I meet on those special occasions or talk long distance," Geraldine explained, "the time we spend together is just so intense. You just don't have a spontaneous discussion about something small and insignificant. I miss that." Geraldine wanted another friend with whom she could talk more often face to face, meet with informally, and do things with occasionally: "I met Alice at several of our monthly professional meetings and we had exchanged visits at our homes, and had gone on a group trip together to see the King Tut exhibition and had such a good time talking on the bus." However, the relationship failed to develop to the level she had hoped it would, considering how compatible she had felt she and Alice were: "I was hoping to get to know her better. We really had a lot in common, but I could pick up that she wasn't cultivating me. I was making all the plans. So I let it drop, but I haven't given up entirely. I had hopes about it and it was a little disappointing. I think of her as kind of a fallow friend who maybe sometime will get cultivated."

It was not altogether surprising that there were many unproductive starts at making friends, since most of the research on "the way people interpret each other's character has painted a depressing picture of partial or total misunderstanding," suggesting that new acquaintances may not see each other particularly clearly (Duck 1981c, 8). Thus it was understandable that first impressions and interpretations of another's behavior might be inaccurate and lead to dead ends in the beginnings of friendship. First impressions often needed correction. Still in Alice's case she had persisted in her search for friends and was looking in particular for couples with whom she and her second husband could associate on their free weekends.

In several cases, if there was no one around who was suitable, the women had made approaches less on the basis of a sense of compatibility than on a gamble that things would turn out better than they appeared at first sight. Whatever the motivations of the moment for voluntarily making a new venture in friendship, it had involved a willingness to devote some resources of time and energy to an unknowable outcome. It was essentially a trial-and-error enterprise, and often a wasteful one. "I am a member of the advisory committee at the local community college," said a think tank administrator.

It's a citizen's committee and there's only one other woman member. I had known her for a number of years through using the employment agency she runs. They recommend good people and I've hired a lot of them. We had become pretty well acquainted over the telephone—we did each other some favors and she even told me about some good prospects for myself—jobs for a personnel director that came across her desk. I'm quite certain that she was the one who recommended me to be a board member.

The first face-to-face meeting of the committee seemed to hold promise for a possible relationship:

Anyway when we finally met, I took to her and suggested we get together for lunch—I said I would be able to combine it with business in Baltimore near her office. But it's never happened, although we keep on mentioning it at the board meetings. All I can gather is that she's not interested in taking it any further. It's getting a little awkward though for me because I guess I felt a little silly being turned down.

Another professional woman told about "how disgusted" she felt with herself when she tried to renew her relationship with another woman who was attending a convention. "When I looked at the list of people attending the convention," she recalled, "I was glad to see Marge's name because I had thought before of trying to get in touch with her again. So as soon as I had unpacked my bags I reached her on the telephone and we arranged to meet in the lobby and have dinner together before the plenary session. She sounded really pleased to hear from me—we had known each other much earlier in our careers, and in a way they paralleled each other but in different areas." There was a lot at stake in this first reunion because of the opportunity it offered to strike up a friendship. "I really thought we had a lot in common. But the most astonishing thing happened when we met in the lobby—she acted as though she didn't know me. I suggested that we could get a drink in the bar first and decide where to have dinner, but she brushed the idea aside. I'll never forget how disgusted I felt about myself imagining that we could become friends."

Despite the costs that were incurred, most of the women were willing to pay them if they believed they could win the prize of a reliable and satisfying friendship. Some, however, had become discouraged by too many unproductive starts and had given up trying to make friends altogether. Others, needing companionship desperately, were driven to cultivating unsuitable friendships. It was not at all infrequent for the women to socialize with each other out of sheer loneliness. Although it was not hard to imagine how it may have happened that some women failed to find desirable partners, it was distressing for them—and embarrassing to remember the details of a bad relationship. Few women volunteered to give accounts of their false starts and their friendships engaged in by default.

Somehow or other friendship is thought to be so commonplace that it has been easy to overlook the complexity of the beginning stages of the process of making friends. Although nearly everyone has succeeded in acquiring some friends, it has been found that many people have trouble taking the first steps in initiating a friendship. Part of the difficulty apparently has stemmed from the fact that meeting new people has been a stressful experience for them. The problems reported by a number of women who had few or no friends were often encountered at the opening of the acquaintanceship. It was possible that they were not only poor at making the original contacts, but also lacked the skills needed for screening out inappropriate choices of people to befriend (Trower 1981).

Indeed, a critical difference in the early stages of a relationship has been found to lie in the possession of some particular social skills. "Social skills seem to be important in the early stages of a relationship—a first filter, if you will—in that people who lack it will not get much further. . . . The process of making friends . . . requires a positive effort and a skilled performance: it is not simply the clicking together of pieces that happened to fit. A person who does not make the effort . . . or whose efforts are so misguided that he or she does everything wrong, will fail to attract anyone" (Cook 1977, 337-338). This need for social skills in interpersonal relationships could help explain why some people had trouble translating acquaintanceships into friendships, while others appear to have mastered the ways of starting new friendships with various degrees of ease and satisfaction.

The terms most often associated with the beginning of a friendship are "choice" and "selection." An emphasis on this kind of decision making has created an image of shopping in a department store where all the items for sale have been put on display so that each piece of merchandise can be pulled off the rack and tried on for size and style. But such comparison shopping for friends was not the way women befriended one another: they did not look for the "best buy" in friends in such a deliberate manner. The process would be more accurately described as easing into friendship, rather than choosing or selecting friends. The skills applied in making successful beginnings were special arts in interpersonal relationships, not calculations of comparative values. These arts had been acquired by the individual during a lifetime of experience, and they reflected the complexity of her whole personality.

Among the middle-class women in this study there were virtuosos at making friends. Although not all of the women were so remarkable that they could be so labeled, at least it could be said about most of them that they had achieved solid accomplishments in the creation of enjoyable and supportive personal friendships and networks of friendly relationships. But the beginnings were always tentative, and the fragility of any friendship in the early stages meant that its survival was never assured. For those that managed to stay alive, there was no guarantee of permanent tenure. How the women nurtured friendship beyond mere acquaintanceship has been presented in the following chapters on the subsequent phases of the natural history of friendship.

NOTES

1. For a discussion of treating strangers as nonpersons, see Lyn H. Lofland, *A World of Strangers: Order and Action in Urban Public Space*, New York: Basic Books, 1973.

2. Ralph Ellison's term "invisible," which he used to describe the protagonist in *The Invisible Man* (New York: Random House, 1952), has come into common usage and is applied to other situations by many who have no knowledge of its origins.

3. Following the tendency of the early sociologists to see urban life as solitary and alienating, Vance Packard made the claim in *A Nation of Strangers* (New York: David McKay, 1972) that there was an absence of deep friendships in modern industrial America.

4. Lyn Lofland drew attention to urban middle- and upper-middle-class women's wide and diverse range of activities and encounters beyond their immediate neighborhoods or communities. See her chapter "The 'Thereness' of Women: A Selective Review of Urban Sociology," in Marcia Millman and Rosabeth Moss Kanter, eds., *Another Voice: Feminist Perspective on Social Life and Social Science*, New York: Anchor Books, 1975.

5. The sections in this chapter on dislike, disregard, and liking criteria in friendship choices have made use of the concepts developed by Miriam J. Rodin, but we have not included a number of the distinctions she developed in her chapter "Non-engagement, Failure to Engage, and Disengagement," in Steve Duck, ed., *Personal Relationships 4: Dissolving Personal Relationships*, New York: Academic Press, 1982.

6. John M. Reisman reviewed the studies of the number of friends people say they have in his chapter on "Adult Friendships," in Steve Duck and Robin Gilmour, eds., *Personal Relationships 2: Developing Personal Relationships*, New York: Academic Press, 1981.

7. Although there was a preponderance of age similarity in the friendship pairs among the respondents, there were also friendships between women of notably divergent ages. For friendship pairs by stage of life, see Marjorie Fiske Lowenthal, Majda Thurnher, and David Chiriboga, *Four Stages of Life: A Comparative Study of Women and Men Facing Transitions*, San Francisco: Jossey-Bass, 1975; Edward A. Powers and G. L. Bultena, "Sex Differences in Intimate Friendships in Old Age," *Journal of Marriage and the Family*, 1976, pp. 739-47; B. Bradford Brown, "A Life-Span Approach to Friendship," in Helena Z. Lopata and David Maines, eds., *Research in the Interweave of Social Roles: Friendship*, Greenwich, CT: JAI Press, 1981.

8. In a chapter on "Boundaries on Interaction," George J. McCall and J. L. Simmons emphasized the many limitations on conceivable interactions between potential role partners such as acquaintances and friends. *Identities and Interactions*, New York: Free Press, 1966. For a contrasting view on the supply of potential friends, see Stanley Milgrim, "The Small World Problem," *Psychology Today*, May 1967, pp. 61-67.

CHAPTER 3

Friendship: Its Substance

> The most pathetic thing in the world is not to have friends to talk to. We speak to each other almost everyday . . . about shopping and such. With a couple of them I talk about the latest books because we are avid readers. And then there are questions about whether life is worth living. You know what? The things I talk to my friends about bore my husband to tears.

For almost all the friendships between the women in the study, talking was central to the relationship. Although most of the women would prefer to share the sum and substance of their daily lives—their routine activities and everyday experiences, their little victories and personal defeats—with the men they were closest to, many found that this was impossible to do. The common experience was that men did not want to hear their comments and speculations about the happenings of the day. Some men acted as if they were paying attention, but more often than not they turned a deaf ear toward the speaker. While conceding that there were some men who were wonderful exceptions to the rule, the women thought that most men felt uncomfortable taking part in discussing the passing scene and the behavior of others. It was usual for men to label such talk "gossip" and decline "on principle" to participate in it. From the women's vantage point there was a gender difference in the universe of discourse that was inhabited by the two sexes. There was a female world of verbal exchange separate and distinct from the male world.[1] So women turned to their women friends as talking companions.

However, there were certain women—a much smaller number—who did not think the talking was the most enjoyable aspect of the time they spent with their friends. For them, doing something together—sharing some recreational activity, developing a sports skill, pursuing a hobby—was the primary focus of the relationship. Their friendship centered around these activities. Such friends were more interchangeable with others than were talking friends. It was easier to replace a sports partner, a quilting enthusiast, or a film buff than a person with whom the core of the relationship was the verbal communication between them.

Besides talking and activity-centered friendships, women also had friends with whom the main tie was the work they did together, whether as employees or as volunteers. In the offices and the various other settings where they spent time doing paid work or donating their services, friends were made as by-products of joint work. Women valued these coworker–collegial friends for qualities in the relationship that might be quite distinct from those in which talking and recreational activities predominated. But often the friends made at work were transformed into talking or activity-centered friends as the relationships developed in the course of the give and take of getting their work done. Some women made their office associates the hub of their social lives, gradually extending the connections with workers beyond the confines of the work setting.

TALKING FRIENDS

The need to talk with friends—women friends—was one that seemed to be taken for granted by virtually all the women. This need was expressed by women who lived in many kinds of circumstances. Whether they stayed at home or worked outside the home, women wanted to spend some of their time talking with other women. There were exceptions—we shall discuss these later—and of course a woman did not have unlimited time away from homemaking or paid employment to devote to her friends. The amount of time available for cultivating friendships was one element in how much the need to talk with friends could be satisfied, although time was not the only variable. Among the women interviewed, it was evident that talking with their friends was seen as particularly important to those women who were at home most of the day or were at work, but single. For women not in the labor force or not members of an intact family or a couple, the possibility of being deprived of friends to talk with was viewed with alarm. A woman who worked part time and whose two adult children were married and living in the vicinity put it this way: "If I didn't have my friends around me, I just couldn't exist. You love your family, you love all of them, but it's just something special that you have to have and without it, it's not a complete life. I feel it in my bones. I just feel it." A housewife who had moved from the city to a suburb said:

> What I would miss most is mainly talking. It isn't the things we do together. We play Mah-Jongg once a week, but we speak to each other almost every day, maybe every other day, and half the time it makes no sense. "I went to New York, and we did this and we saw that show and we had dinner," and she would even tell me the menu, and I'll listen and I find myself saying the same kind of things to her. We discuss other more serious matters, too, all kinds of problems in our lives and bigger issues about world events.

There were women talkers of many varieties—those who were the good conversationalists and those at the opposite extreme who talked a great deal but never exchanged ideas. There were those who were shy and quiet in mixed company but opened up in the comfortable presence of a good friend. It seemed important to have at least one female friend with whom it was possible to arrange time for face-to-face talking or a relaxed telephone conversation. In many instances the women had developed a primary relationship with one or two other women by keeping in touch with them and communicating about everyday matters without needing to watch every word they spoke for fear of misinterpretation.[2] A suburban professional woman with a crowded schedule—she taught part time at a university, was the mother of three, and considered her husband her best friend—still took time to make friends in a new neighborhood. She explained why:

Why do I do that? I don't know, but I really think I need a good friend. Just to talk to somebody. About the little moans and groans, like why doesn't your husband pick up his stuff. Things like that, things that you can't even say to your sister. Edna, she'll tell me things she can't talk about with other people, like her niece took off and was living with some guy and they were just frantic. I haven't had any great big problems, but I've talked to her about my own relatives' problems, and I know it won't go any further.

A young single woman who was a newly appointed member of a history department excused herself for sounding "corny" when she referred to her friends on campus: "A day without talking with my friends," she said, "is a day without sunshine." She went on to explain how much she depended on being in touch with her friends:

We all do very solitary work, all of us. Although people think of the teaching profession as sociable, it isn't. My work is really solitary, essentially lonely. We all have separate offices, places to be alone, because we have to be by ourselves to do our work. I was finishing a book manuscript this spring and I didn't see anyone as much as usual or talk to them as much as usual. They'd call and say, "Are you all right?" and I'd say, "Yes, I'm on page three hundred twenty-two." It's really important to me to have these friends, almost as an antidote against my work, which is extremely singular.

So the time, the amount of time, we spend together goes in cycles. It doesn't have the same intensity level all the time, but it's pretty intense most of the time. When I'm not up against a deadline, we'll be on the phone several times a day, at least twice a day with Virginia and the same with Debbie. You're so busy you can't spend enough time with anyone, actual time as opposed to time on the telephone, but no day goes by without at least checking and hearing each other's voice.

A woman in her late forties whose husband spent a great deal of time overseas on business recognized how much she relied on her friends. She compared her attachment to her friends with the pattern of association that she observed in a woman who had recently moved into the house next to hers:

We have a new neighbor next door—she doesn't have any friends. She comes from a large family and she feels that with family, sisters, and children, that's enough. I disagree. I find that sometimes I can confide more in a friend than I can in family because even with your children, they have their own lives and they'll get married and you're not included basically, so if you put your whole life and friendship in your children and they leave you, then where are you? The thing about a friend is that with a good friend, you may not see them every day and talk, but you know if you need them, if there is some real trouble, you can call on them.

For this woman, like many others, the value of a good friend went far beyond the pleasure of mere sociability. She counted on her friend for guidance and comfort when she was facing difficulties. She felt there was someone she could call and talk to openly when she wanted to air a personal problem and was confident that she would be listened to when she needed to talk. With a really good friend, she would not feel uncomfortable later on about what she had said. In addition, she thought that her friends turned to her to bounce off ideas and to get some help for solving problems by talking them over with her. Talking with a friend was one of the best ways to alleviate feelings of loneliness and depression (Jong-Gierveld 1985). "I really go to Sybil for refreshment and nourishment," Marie said, as she spoke about her monthly lunches with her friend of more than forty years. "I can talk about things freely with her and I tell her things I would never mention to anyone else. I think of her as my alter ego."

The other side of talking was listening, and being a listener was not always easy or convenient. "There are burdens to the relationship with Nam, who is my best friend," said Molly, who had been Nam's roommate at college, where they became very good friends. After graduation they decided to move to a Midwestern city, where they shared an apartment and pursued successful careers in business and social work, respectively. As a corporate sales manager, Molly had to spend a good many days a month on the road traveling. When she was home her social life was centered around Nam and their group of friends. Although devoted to Nam, Molly found some of the obligations of the friendship taxing:

I think the heaviest obligation for me is time. You give up time for a good friend. With Nam I spend time listening to her when I know she wants to talk about something, and that takes a lot of time. It is time I would rather devote to something else. Right now I am getting ready for the CPA and I need study time desperately, but with a close friend you are willing to spend the time listening, and I guess it must balance out in the end because she does that for me at some other time.

A number of the women said they had turned to their friends, rather than to family members, when they wanted to talk about their troubles, and their friends had done the same with them. A married woman confessed that if she had a serious personal problem she needed to air, she always chose to confide in a close friend rather than her husband.

I would talk it over with one of my close friends, not my husband. Being frightfully honest, if he ever heard me say that, he would die that I wouldn't turn to him first because I am sure he would to me. There are a lot of things I don't feel I can talk about with him that I can discuss with the women I know well. The peace needs to be maintained at home. There's a lot of "Don't rock the boat" or sort of a decorum around here, both of us having been through rather horrendous marriages. We are very nice to each other and we talk about the things people talk about. It never gets terribly heavy. We don't fight.

The women said that a warning signal went up when the usual amount of time a friend spent talking with them dropped off noticeably. Martha was one of a trio of compatible friends living in the same community. Occasionally she felt some pangs of jealousy when she suspected that Jane and Claudette were seeing more of each other than of her:

If Jane neglects to come in on her usual rounds and goes to Claudette's all the time, I question her. Then she'll tell me, "Well, Martha, you said I couldn't stay too long the last time I dropped in, so I thought you were busy with your writing and didn't want to be interrupted." When this happens I think we try to be honest about asking for an explanation. We try not to hurt each other even unintentionally. I'll be the first one to march over to Claudette's and say, "All right, what's going on?"

Shirley and Lynn were close friends who had met at their jobs as researchers at a major behavioral consulting firm on the West

Coast. When Lynn began a new relationship with a man, she spent less time talking with Shirley. "But that was okay," Shirley said, "because we talked about it once. When you're in a new relationship, that happens, and that's okay, we're comfortable with it."

> Once when Shirley asked me, "Are you mad at me for something?" I was surprised that she asked because I wasn't conscious of being angry. But I realize she's extra alert to any signs that I may feel neglected by seeing less of her. You see, we're close enough that I know what's going on. We may not spend as much time together, but I've never had any feeling of Lynn's being unavailable. If I wanted to call her up and say, "I want to claim an evening," I could have it any time. There's no question that we both need some time to talk and I must have shown I felt sort of deprived without realizing it.

The talking engaged in on a regular basis and on a wide variety of subjects did not necessarily lead to more than a superficial relationship. A number of homebound women said they had grabbed onto other women to talk to mostly as a way of passing the hours that hung heavy on their hands, for example, in the early child-rearing years. Sometimes, the talking between such mothers was merely a series of casual encounters that provided some release from the boredom of having to be with their babies and preschoolers all day long. About the talking that went on in the laundry room of her apartment building, a new mother in her mid-thirties commented:

> Even though you meet the same mothers and children over and over again and spend hours on end talking, you don't necessarily meet with people you want to become friends with. You are with people in the basement while you are washing your clothes and your kids start playing together. The relationship between the mothers is not based on who you are, but on how close you live to each other and whether the kids get along. It's a matter of convenience more than being attracted to someone and choosing them as friends.

Predictably, the long sessions of talking between such neighbors enabled the women to share many aspects of daily life. These relationships of convenience—the conversations and exchanges between chance neighbors—filled a real need and were valued while they lasted. In addition, sometimes all that talk led to the deepening of a passing acquaintanceship into a close friendship that lasted beyond merely tolerated association in laundry rooms, parks, and backyards.

The polite greetings that occurred when neighbors' paths occasionally crossed had developed into conversation continued over a lifetime. Of course the opportunity for some sort of interaction was crucial for the formation of women's friendships. Studies of housing projects have shown that friendships were often dependent on accidents of geography. People were most likely to become friends with those women they saw most frequently, often by virtue of mere physical arrangements.[3] A widow in her early sixties told about her upstairs neighbor, Molly:

> She lived in the apartment above me and we were very, very close. In fact, her children were the same ages as mine and all the kids, hers and mine, were born there. We spent a lot of the day together, and at night she would knock on the pipe and say, "Come on up. We feel like having coffee and cake." Or, if I'd hear her walking overhead after the children were in bed, I'd say, "Why don't you come down and have a cup of coffee?" We're still very, very close after forty years, even though I moved to the suburbs.

Talking, then, was central to virtually all the friendships described by the women in the study. If the buzz of Woman Talk could be raised a few decibels, it would be a deafening hum throughout the land. And if women could have their druthers, that sound would be much louder—there would be much more of it than there is. If there were more time for talking with friends, women would be glad of it.[4]

Woman Talk

Woman Talk is a special art. Whether engaged in at home, in the office, across the lunch table, or over the telephone, its distinguishing characteristic is the ordinariness of a good deal of the subject matter it includes. It is not usually about world-shaking events, nor does it often consist of deep probings into the personal problems and tender psyches of the speakers. Women talk about almost everything, including how they feel and what they think about issues of broad significance, but the daily fare is apt to be pretty plain and concerned with seemingly mundane, inconsequential subjects. That is what makes it an art. It requires the ingenuity of writing an essay on pins—not much to work with and therefore a challenging assignment. An interesting elaboration of the topic makes demands on the imagination and the creative skills if nothing is to be made into something.

One of the main functions of Woman Talk is entertainment. The routinest of incidents may be given a slant in the telling to make it diverting. Women make a good try at keeping life interesting for each other when, as they put it, they tell each other "all this foolishness." It so happens that "this foolishness," whether it occurs at home or elsewhere, fills most of the hours of life of any person who is not in the throes of creative invention, decision making, or professional practice.

The art of good Woman Talk lies in the recounting of the event in a way that makes it memorable. A friend, like any storyteller, builds a solid knowledge of the characters, setting the plot by piling detail on detail, adding touches of humor and pathos, direct and indirect quotations, and other literary flourishes, interpreting along the way. Some women are experts at this, but most have a reasonably good grasp of the art. It is a woman's stock in trade. Women appreciate the vividness of the mundane fact, the lasting impact of repetition, the fascination of understanding motives, the thrill of abstract comparisons. Knowledge conveyed by one woman to another about the people, things, places, events, attitudes, and feelings experienced constructs for herself and her friend a picture of the world—made more comprehensible when put into words.

Because Woman Talk takes up almost any subject matter that can be commented on, a good friend knows a surprisingly lot about her friend's daily life and her views on a variety of questions. Among friends, there is a gradual accumulation of information about the other person's personal and family life, but it is a knowledge gained through the eyes and ears of the friend and is therefore mostly from the friend's subjective perspective (Altman and Taylor 1973). By and large the friend knows about her friend's life not so much through direct experience with what is happening to her, but through what she is told. Unlike a family member, a friend does not usually witness such regular routines as getting up in the morning and preparing breakfast or the hours spent keeping house. Consequently she can know these aspects of her life only vicariously. Glimpses into the backstage of a friend's life are, by definition, rather uncommon and limited (Goffman 1959).

What substitutes for the direct experience is the talking and the fact that Woman Talk has a dynamic of its own. If it were the case that women were in full control of the process, then it might be that one woman would tell the other only what she wanted the other to know and no more. She would project an image of herself and her family in the best light, interpret events of the past and developments in the making to her best advantage, give consistent and informed views on topics of interest and importance. Some women succeed in maintaining this kind of vigilance, this distance from other women.

But talk among women who are friends does not operate this way (Schlenker 1984). The relaxed conditions under which friends converse and the dynamic of Woman Talk encourage a gradual and uncensored revelation of information and feelings. After a while there are times when friends are off guard. The story of the other person's life begins to fit together as intricately as a jigsaw puzzle. The pieces are made up of descriptions of experiences, people, events, activities, feelings, judgments, philosophies, and beliefs. The more pieces that are placed, the clearer the picture becomes. If some of the pieces don't fit in, the image is blurred. Of course what it all means is up to the observer—the friend who has been given the pieces, who has been supplied with the running history of the life of her friend and is in a position to look at the emerging picture. Over a period of years women go about acquainting their friends with many of the nooks and crannies of their lives. Talking is the conduit of the relationship through which information between friends flows. Although the other senses of seeing and touching are used and make a contribution to knowing another person, hearing what another woman says is by far the most critical sense for tuning into another individual's life.

Good friends know that certain subjects are off limits (Miell 1984). They reserve the privilege of privacy and grant it to others. For many, the family finances, for example, are a taboo area. A friend may know almost everything about another woman's personal life, even to the extent of being acquainted in some detail about troubles between spouses, yet never hear a word about money matters, except in general terms. Of course the standard of living that a friend maintains conveys some definite indicators about her income. If there are disparities between friends in this regard, talking about them may be painful and disparaging. For some good friends the line is also drawn at talking about the relationship with the men they are close to. A friend, for example, may consider this a taboo area to enter even though she knows that a friend's husband or lover is "cheating on her." Withholding such information was justified by some women in the study on several grounds, some of which were related to fears of endangering the friendship and norms of nonintervention in the personal problems of others (Turner 1952; Mayer 1957). What is left out of the communication between friends is probably less significant than the broad scope of what is included, even though they practice self-restraint on touchy subjects. As a result, it is likely that a good friend, in many cases, could give a fuller and more accurate portrait of a friend than even some members of her family could draw. At least she would have her own compendium of information, some of which may be confidences with which she alone had been entrusted.

In studies measuring the amount of talking that goes on between husbands and wives in middle-class America, it has been found that there is an astonishingly small amount of it and that much of it is impersonal (Bernard 1981). The middle-class man—who spends his working day at the office and is routinely away from home and wife for nine to twelve hours, on the average, engages in direct conversation with her for only about twenty minutes a week, usually in spurts of several minutes' duration. This finding is hard to believe but must be looked at carefully within terms of the definition used for "direct conversation," which excludes talk addressed to children, pets, and spoken to no one in particular: such comments as "What's for dinner?" "Has the dog been fed?" "Why are these toys in the middle of the living room?" If the man happens to be of the talkative type, he may keep his wife up to date on developments at the office, but in these circumstances the wife is usually listening to a report, mirroring the husband's feelings, and not doing much of the talking herself (Lofland

1973). If she tries to, she often finds he is only half listening. Some women who had discovered this about men spoke of confronting them with it. One young woman told about such an encounter:

> Eventually I got out what I was trying to say, although at first I hurt his feelings by jumping on him. . . . I guess that the things that were bothering me were that when I talked to him, he didn't hear me. . . . I told him that all the things he hated about his father were exactly what he was turning into. When his father was speaking with you, he never heard what you said back to him. . . . I guess I had mentioned this to him briefly before, complaining to him and asking him to pay attention to what I was saying. I guess, like his father, he wasn't paying attention then either. Of course it is not just something that is peculiar to him. To hell with it, you might as well be talking to the wall. You get the same response. I can't be bothered with men like that. I don't have time for that.

Thus many wives and lovers found that their partners either did not engage in much conversation with them or did all the talking themselves and little of the listening. For women, this was one aspect of their subordination to men that had taught them to be facilitators in conversation, asking the appropriate question, making the judicious probe, maintaining eye contact, laughing and assenting, and, when proposing a new topic, introducing it in the form of a question rather than as a positive statement (Thorne and Henley 1975). Such conversational styles were seldom used by men, but most women practiced them deftly and quite unconsciously when talking with men. Research on mixed-sex conversations has shown that the men do more of the talking and at times and on topics of their own choice (Frank and Anshen 1983). A young draftswoman recounted how she challenged men who were in the habit of interrupting her in mid-sentence:

> I don't feel I can sit down and really have an honest conversation with a man, especially with many of the men I work with. They won't let you get in a word edgewise. They'll talk right over you. They'll interrupt you in mid-stream when you are trying to get a thought out. They'll cut you right off. I would deliberately do it to them and then say, "Oh, you don't like it, do you? It is okay when you do it to me, but I can't do it back." And then they say, "Oh, you're so defensive," and I say, "No,

I'm not. I'm just trying to be a person." But they really don't understand what's happening.

The women needed to be this assertive and to possess superior verbal skills in order "to get in a word edgewise." A woman in her early sixties described the difficulties she had when talking with her husband. He had recently retired from upper-level management of a major corporation and was enthusiastically described by his wife as a good marriage partner. "The trouble is he's a perfectionist," she explained. "He's very critical of what I say, stops me in the middle before I finish, so what I need is someone with whom I can talk without being constantly criticized. Another thing I don't think a man knows how to do too well is to listen to you, and that is what I need occasionally. I need someone who will listen to me."

People in subordinate positions—slaves, servants, employees, and women—have historically learned to humor the masters around whom they had to watch their words, disguise their feelings, listen attentively without being listened to, and suffer the insults of language full of classist, racist, and sexist vocabulary (Thorne and Henley 1975; Kramarae 1981). Behind their backs they all talked freely and made fun of the overlords and overladies; the servants gossiped downstairs about the family upstairs; the slaves and cleaning women mimicked the ladies of the house; the workers griped about their bosses; and the women turned to their women friends to talk about their lives on an equal footing, free of linguistic sexism.

The difference between woman/woman pairs and woman/man pairs in conversation was that the female combination had usually worked out a kind of "equal time" arrangement. Over the long run each person was allotted time to talk and expected to grant some rough equivalent, although not necessarily an exactly equal, amount of talking time. In addition, a woman frequently was attentive to what was being said by another woman, did not interrupt her, and stored the information in her memory. Even though the immediate response might not have seemed fully adequate to the meaning of the information and feelings being conveyed, women expected someone whom they had chosen as a friend to listen to them talk. The friendship was a kind of talking–listening compact. Implicit understandings developed in regard to the amounts and kinds of information and emotions that would be disclosed. It was not necessarily a rigidly established or perfectly symmetrical level of verbal exchange—it seemed to ebb and flow in an ongoing relationship according to the immediate circumstances of each friend's life. Whatever expectations they had developed for carrying out the role of being a friend and having a friend, they knew that they wanted to talk to another person and be listened to by her. Because of what was said and what was remembered, obligations were incurred and plans made for the future. The talking–listening compact was undertaken seriously between good friends.

ACTIVITY-CENTERED FRIENDSHIPS

Many friendships did not start and continue so much on the basis of talking as that of sharing an activity enjoyed and participated in by both women.[5] This did not mean that a lot of talking did not go on before, during, and after the activity, but as explained by one woman,

> I am not the coffee-klatching type. My friends tend to be activity oriented. . . . I have a number of friends, but what we have in common is some activity. . . . I need friends, I need people who will do interesting things with me, not who will be great confidantes. . . . At each place we've lived I've plunged into different things. . . . On the first campus I had a great circle of friends, all with similar interests—we were all very active in the faculty wives' club, in a bridge club, I still go and substitute in a bridge club twenty-five years later.

This woman had a model in her mother, who had centered a number of lifelong friendships around sports.

> When we moved to another city and into the business world where there was no organized structure to fit into like the faculty women's club, I decided to take diving lessons, and out of those women nutty enough to start taking diving lessons after age thirty, my closest friends evolved. We weren't neighbors; we came from all over the city, seven of us, and this was the focal point of my week, this diving class. My mother had a group of friends just like mine, all her life.

Friendships made by this woman always started around a specific activity, and they spread into many other areas of interest:

> Later we got together to do other things after our coach got busier teaching Olympic stars instead of us old ladies. We would prepare gourmet luncheons for each other, we would go cross-country skiing, water skiing, play tennis—eventually we took sailing lessons. None of us are weak women. This was the kind of woman who would hitch the boat to the car herself, back it out of the driveway, and launch it. We were all very strong and with a lot of energy, each one very active in volunteer work of different kinds, the blind, Girl Scouts, the church.

She continued to talk about new friends found during the course of her recreational and service activities:

> I have made new friends here now, and they are tied into activities I have. I have just discovered a gal on the board of our YMCA. So much of my time is compartmentalized into activities; I have next to no time of my own that isn't committed. I have played tennis this morning, will go to work at the School for the Deaf at noon, and at four o'clock someone is picking me up to make salads for the church supper. My friends are involved in these activities, but some of the women are just acquaintances, like at the church this afternoon. I'll enjoy working with her, but we'll be just acquaintances.

Talking went on in all the activities engaged in by this woman and her friends, and, as she described the difference between whether a person became a friend or merely an acquaintance in the course of playing a tennis match or doing volunteer work, it was a matter of whether she and the other woman "clicked from the start." Still the core of the friendship centered around an activity or a series of activities that were undertaken together and with other women. But the coffee-klatching—the talking for the sake of talking—never became the *raison d'être* for the relationship.

Friendships made by some of the women, then, had begun in the course of doing something together—a specific activity—and then spread out to engaging in other activities and talking about many other areas. The women in the study had a wide array of such interests. A woman with many interests reflected on her notion that she "would probably have many more friends and spend much more time with them" if she and her husband did not have so many of the same things they liked to do together. They had made a point of keeping up in a marginal way with each other's interests so that "each one of us can sort of go along with the other, say he with my photography, me with his favorite sports, as an intelligent companion, not a blooming idiot." Speaking of friends other than her husband, she commented: "I've come to think about friends differently. I used to think that friends were for all seasons, that when one looked for a friend, one looked for someone who was compatible across all areas, but I no longer think that way. . . . Now I have friends for different things." In describing the "different things" involved in these friendships, she specified particular activities as the core of the friendship:

> I have a friend who's very interesting for me to talk to. He's fairly well read and we disagree on a lot of issues, but he's really my friend for doing woodworking projects, carpentry. We had this great compatibility in that we both liked to work with our hands, and we liked to talk about building things and worry over design issues, and go around and look at stuff and dream about making up build-it-yourself furniture. That was the entree and then we became sort of more general friends.

Another woman had a friend who had been a coworker in a research center but had left to take a position in city government. It was after their separation from a common workplace that the friendship really flourished: "I guess Gena is interested in modern painting, although she doesn't take it very seriously. Anyway, she would call me up from time to time and mention exhibits and so we go around to them together, and she doesn't know as much about the history of art as I do, so my role is to provide some of the background. We also swim together regularly."

It would be difficult to say with any certainty how much emphasis on engaging in an activity with a friend versus mainly "just talking" set these women's friendships apart from most other women's. But the distinctions made by both of them were not made by others. There seemed to be a difference in the goal they expected to achieve in the relationship. For one of these women, this was stated in her own words explicitly. "I need friends. I need people who will do interesting things with me, not who will be great confidantes." For the other, it had been a matter of coming to the realization that she should not "think that friends were for all seasons . . . but for different things," and usually for engaging in a particular activity that reflected a strong interest they shared. Rather, it was a quite specific undertaking that usually involved some background of knowledge and skills and that almost, by definition, would be engaged in by the individual over the long term whether or not this particular partner had been found to do it with. If one person could not be found to join in the activity, then someone else could be corralled and with any luck and with the shared enjoyment of learning to dive, doing woodworking or whatever, the second person had the potential for being as good an "activity friend" as the first.

Making friends by way of shared activities, it should be quickly pointed out, had not worked out for everybody. As a matter of fact, some of the women who were searching for friends and had hoped to find a friend through a shared activity were met with disappointment. Acting on the notion that joining a tennis club, for example, was a way of finding friends among the players was spoken about as an unproductive blind alley for friendship formation, according to a middle-aged divorcée:

> We get our reservation for the court, play the game, singles or doubles, sometimes have an ice tea together, and that's it. Sure, we might get to know the names of our kids and carry on with some chit-chat but there's nothing beyond that. The game is the reason for being there. People are always suggesting that I do things with other women and I'll make friends that way, but it doesn't work out for me. What can I get into, what activity or organization where I will make friends?

An older woman with a special talent for friendship described her regular golf foursome as "just sociable companions, really acquaintances, not actually friends, though I've played with them a couple a days a week for many, many summers. You don't talk when you play golf and tennis, so acquaintanceship is about as far as it goes." The issue of whether a shared activity had promoted, or at least allowed for, talking was addressed directly by a woman who was describing the efforts she had made to make friends as she moved from city to city when the company her husband was working for assigned him to locations in various parts of its East Coast operation: "Most of our friends we made at that next to last move—and we are still near enough to them to see them often—were attached to either the amateur theater we got involved in or Great Books." She gave her reasoning for thinking that certain kinds of activities were likely to lead to friendship:

> I made more intimate friends through Great Books than in the theater group. You get very close to someone when you discuss their opinions on books and ideas. It was really difficult when we would enter a town. It was hard to find someone because it had to click. Great Books was marvelous for me at that point—that's already going on thirty years ago. My idea is that you really have to go out and find your group first, and in that group, which was Great Books for us, I found that as we talked, there were as many as four or five of us who just seemed to talk more to each other. We began to hang out together and pretty soon it got down to a one-to-one basis without a feeling of having left anyone out. It's a very fast way of making friends.

Another woman who had also moved a great deal had discovered that getting into activities that required talking was best for friendship formation: "One thing I did was to take art lessons," she explained, "and you get involved with others interested in art. What is special about painting is that you talk while you are painting and then eventually the class met in our house. The man who was our teacher is still around and a good friend and a wonderful guy."

As families were moved from city to city by business transfers or entered strange neighborhoods when they purchased a new house, the women often tried the route of taking part in an activity or joining an organization in their search for new friends. Sometimes they joined a local chapter of a national women's club of which they had been active members before moving, for example, the American Association of University Women, the Radcliffe College Alumnae Association, the P.E.O. (a women's lodge). About the latter group, a chapter member said, "I have no fear of moving because I know that club members will welcome me wherever I go. It's a very friendly group." Others made their way to the Newcomer Clubs, which offered a variety of planned activities to people who were new to their communities. Frequently the motive for participating in such a program was to meet people and only minimally to take part in the activity itself. When joining a club happened to work out well as a means to finding friends, the newly created pairs of friends often dropped the activity altogether and concentrated on the friendships they had been looking for. On the other hand, while some of these new friendships flourished independently of the activity that had brought them together, others were sufficiently imbedded in the organization that they carried on a mixture of a talking and activity-centered friendship. As one illustration, this had happened to friends made during church work together, inasmuch as a religious faith and the common bond of their religious affiliation had been important elements of their friendship. In another instance women who had met at a stained glass-making class said their friends had to be equally engrossed in the hobby or they would never see each other.

One suburban housewife who had postponed having children until she had worked as a professional social worker through her late twenties found herself very much alone when she moved to a development of single-family dwellings. It turned out that her immediate neighbors were older than she was, had teenage children, and were away all day at jobs, so she not only saw little of them, but also had almost nothing in common with them. Deciding that she had to do something about getting involved with other women, she began attending several of the interest groups at the local temple. In time she made three good friends, each one very different from the other and each supplying something special that rounded out her life and allayed her initial intense loneliness. Although she and her friends still attended the meetings and took part in many of the organized activities, as well as going to the temple services regularly, the center of the friendships had shifted from shared activities to talking. She and her friends met occasionally for lunch at a restaurant so they could talk without being interrupted by the children. However, the most frequent contact was made over the telephone: "The telephone has become a major part of my life. I find that when you are by yourself with a young child, you need relief. You need a time when you can talk to another person. I would say that with these three people, I talk with them at least three or four times a week, sometimes daily."

What friends did together has been described by the women in the study along this talking—activity axis with a variety of permutations tipping in favor of one direction or the other. The women had different styles of seeking what they wanted from their friends and what they intended to give in return. During the development of a friendship the women engaged in a kind of private negotiation to arrive at how their relationship would be conducted. In contrast with kin and work relationships, there was a great measure of autonomy in friendship, both in the original decision to develop the relationship and in the way it was carried on. "I think I have gotten pretty coldhearted in my old age," admitted a forty-year-old opinion analyst:

> I used to be the person everyone came to with their problems. Blub, blub, blub, always this huge deluge. I think I've finally learned to choose my friends for what they have to give me. That sounds dreadful, I know, but I think that someone just needing you isn't enough. For me it works out better if they have something I need in return. Superficially, things like camaraderie, and maybe some spontaneity. When I call up and say, "I really feel like going out to lunch today," and they say, "Okay, I'll drop everything." The same with going to movies, restaurants, and plays, so you can call up and say, "Let's get tickets to so-and-so and have dinner in New York."
>
> With my good friends the time they want to spend with me and the things they're interested in doing usually seem to be the same as mine. For my closest friends, the three of them, they like to sit around and talk *with* me, not *at* me.

As far as what was preponderant in their immediate thoughts about their friendships, the talking end of the axis got by far the greatest weight by almost all the women. But there were variations in the combinations of the two elements in terms of how they were valued and what amount of time was devoted to each one. Some women have found friends through activities and then pursued the relationships quite independently of the activities. For a few others, there seemed to be a kind of friendship specialization connecting one friend to another. In these friendships the activities made up the core of the relationship around which other activities might develop and "just talk" might eventually ensue. In the main, though, activities were barely mentioned in the interviews when women spoke freely about their friendships. It was as though they had literally never been engaged with a friend in anything but the interpersonal relationship itself, and although this might have involved eating at the friend's house, doing some errands with her, going to a club meeting, or going out to the theater with two other couples, these were regarded as mere details of living, parts of a personal economy that served as a neutral background to the central focus of the friendship, which was talking. Anything else that might take place was not uppermost in their minds. In fact, the talking was what was most dearly valued.

WORK FRIENDS

Besides talking and activity-oriented friendships, the women also had friends with whom the principal feature of the relationship was working together. This could be on the job or in civic organizations where they worked as volunteers. There appeared to be some special characteristics of friendships carried on while engaged in making a living or spending time regularly doing various kinds of work in community organizations of many sorts. In these settings friends were made as by-products of performing some kind of work together, and women valued these coworker–collegial friends for qualities in the relationships that were quite distinct from those in which talking and recreational activities predominated. When they were in the middle of changing jobs, women said they regarded the new group of people they expected to associate with as a potential source of companionship and even good friendships. Because most of the waking hours of women who were employed outside their homes were spent on the job, they had the opportunity to become better acquainted with coworkers than with most other people. For working women, both personal and collegial friends were normally made in the work place. "Where else am I going to meet people?" Of course there were disappointments. Sometimes none of their workmates proved to be good prospects for friendship. Many times the relationships did not progress beyond acquaintanceships and ceased to exist soon after a coworker had left for a new job. They found they had nothing in common once they no longer had the same people and problems—and office politics—to talk about, but during the time they had worked together they had enjoyed each other's company and occasionally felt quite close. Some women managed to cultivate good friends at work and kept being friends with them after job changes by lunching together, talking on the telephone, and getting together in their free time. Many enduring friendships were started between women who happened to be thrown together at work.

My Friend, the Volunteer

Just how these coworker–collegial friends actually differed from the more traditional close friends of women was explored by Gouldner in a study of middle-class women who were active in the League of Women Voters in the 1950s (Gouldner 1959). At that time middle-class women had not yet entered the labor force to the extent they have today. But a certain proportion of the upper-middle-class women who had the leisure to devote to civic and philanthropic work did so on an almost full-time basis and with a seriousness easily equivalent to being in a salaried occupation. As a method of finding out something about the characteristics of friendships made while working on serious volunteer projects, a sample of the active members in a Los Angeles chapter were interviewed. First, they were asked to name their "closest" friend in the organization and then they answered a series of questions about the nature of the friendship. The women immediately began to draw distinctions among the various types of friendships they had with the women they knew in the League. Many of them asked, "What kind of friend do you mean? Do you want working friends or social friends?" Or, "Well, I feel closest to Margaret, but Trudy and I see each other a lot more in the League." The concept of "closest friend" in the League meant different things to different women, and the findings culled from their answers and observations helped clarify some distinctions between women's friends at work and their more traditional close friends.

Although the members made use of a number of different criteria in accounting for their choice of their "closest friend," they did not emphasize the work they did together when describing the kind of relationship they had with their closest friend in the organization. In fact, they pointed out immediately that "closest friends" saw each other socially at home and other places, not just at League meetings. Specifically they mentioned being able to talk over personal problems with each other and freely share confidences. Knowing the other woman as an individual, sharing the personal details of the other's life, feeling free to call up spontaneously just to chat on the telephone—these were the aspects of the relationship that were emphasized. It appeared that when a friendship blossomed and extended beyone the boundaries of the organization, it became less restrained and more informal, and a feeling of intimacy began to develop. As one woman explained, "at first the friendship was on an intellectual basis, talking about League issues and so forth, but now it is much more down to earth. We discuss the children's problems and husbands, and go to each other with problems in a helpful spirit." Another woman said her closest friend in the League "helps me blow off steam—which is what a friend is for, I think. She was my safety valve in a time of trouble a while back." One after another the women drew a picture of a talking friendship.

However, in addition to these personal friends, they had made friends of another kind in the course of working with other members on various organizational projects. A variety of terms were used to refer to such women—they were called "working" friends, "non-social" friends, and sometimes plain "good" friends. Even if they were not on intimate terms with these good, non-social, working friends, they enjoyed the working aspect of the relationship enormously. They felt loyal to them, a feeling that appeared to develop in the course of sharing a kind of organizational intimacy rather than a personal intimacy. This consisted of many things. It consisted of sharing many quite private and personal views about the organization. The women in the League derived a great deal of satisfaction from expressing views about goals and tactics, strengths and weaknesses of their own chapter, and assessments of the leadership and programs of the national organization. This meant that they talked frequently and often heatedly about organizational problems instead of so much about their own lives and private concerns. They got into the habit of rehashing meetings over coffee, joking about the amusing episodes they had been through together and the embarrassing faux pas they had committed. They called on their working friends for organizational help and solicited support for weathering organizational storms. Most of all they felt a real obligation to "do well" on projects they undertook, partly because they knew their friends were counting on them. All this interaction with their working friends reinforced their own growing enthusiasm for the organization.

When asked to describe the history of these friendships, the women referred much more often to growth of mutual respect rather than to the development of intimacy. A dominant element in the attraction between working friends was admiration. "She's just a fantastic organizer. You should see her with the members of the legislature." There was bragging about another woman's exceptional skills: "She's as good or better than the rest of the high-powered lobbyists up there." They said that they "liked each other," "knew each other best," "thought a great deal of her," but the terms "closeness" and "intimacy" were not usually applied to working friends. There was also some honest criticism. Searching for a term to summarize the elements of these relationships, it seemed that "task-oriented friendships" might be one way of describing them, since the main focus of such a friendship was on work and the individual's contribution to it.

The discovery of the importance of task-oriented friendship in organizational settings led to looking at the possibility of the developmental sequence in the making of these friendships. It turned out that it was often intimate, or at least "social," friends who had introduced the women to the organization and gotten them started on their organizational careers, as in the case of a woman who had said, "Well, you know, I just can't turn down June when she asks me to do something." What June had requested was that her friend attend a League meeting with her. In other words, the close friend had been the one to recruit her to membership by issuing an invitation she did not feel free to refuse.

The task-oriented friendships were developed later, both through actual participation in activities and through introductions from other friends. Once developed, these relationships became one of the potent forces inducing commitment to the work of the organization, and indeed at some point the friendships and the commitment became mutually supportive. Once she had made some commitment to the group goals, the individual was given jobs to do, and there was pressure on her to do them well. She now had so much invested in these goals that she almost always chose other members to work with on the basis of whether she could rely on them to do the particular task well. Those women whose performance on projects had gained her respect became her good friends in the organization, and in turn reinforced her own involvement in its aims. In the words of one of the most highly committed members, "I lost interest in people who are not interested in the League, and the better the members they are, the more I feel involved with them." Another member said, "We now have a common bond in the League, and it has made our friendship much more meaningful."

At first it was surprising to discover that the women who were task-oriented friends engaged in only limited socializing with each other outside of their chapter activities. This was different from the usual pattern of development in women's friendships. Once a friendship had begun, it ordinarily progressed to the stage of being more diffuse—meaning that more and different kinds of things were done together.[6] However, among the women who regarded each other as work friends, this did not happen. In fact, they seldom saw each other beyond the boundaries of the organizational work. Between them, the primary bond was the work they did together in the organization.

Of course there was always the possibility that good working friendships would develop into intimate ones, particularly after the women had survived some organizational wars together. The danger that this would happen and be detrimental to the work of the organization was recognized by some of the officers. They knew that keeping work "businesslike" and acting "professional" were somewhat elusive goals. But in the distinctions made by members between their closest friends in the organization and their working friends, the active members indicated quite clearly that they had found two kinds of friendship: the one of a personal, intimate sort; the other, a good and satisfying work relationship. They valued both types very much and for different reasons and hoped they would continue to have friends of both kinds.

Friends on the Job

Since the 1950s, when the data were gathered about the League of Women Voters volunteers, there has been a dramatic shift of women into the labor force. The influx had begun earlier; the percentage of employed women picked up momentum in the early 1940s at the time women took jobs in the war plants when the men left for military service. At the end of World War II many of these women returned to their homes, but the trend for women to work was not reversed and eventually they entered the paid workforce in greater numbers than men. In the decade of the 1970s women accounted for about thirteen million of the increase in new civilian workers compared with roughly nine million men. At the beginning of the 1980s the trend continued upward. More than 52 percent of all women of working age were in the labor force in 1981 compared with 43 percent in 1970 (U.S. Bureau of the Census, 1984). This amounted to a total of some forty-seven million women. The majority of these women had no other option but to go to work, since almost all of them used their earnings to either support themselves or maintain their family's basic needs.

The situation of working women was this: 42 percent of the women were unmarried and self-supporting; another 29 percent were married to men making less than $10,000 a year, and therefore had to work in order to keep a decent standard of living (U.S. Bureau of the Census, 1981). Most of the women earned modest wages—by far the greatest number of women were employed in low-paying unskilled jobs. Of those who made a living in white-collar occupations, most were clerks, service workers, and secretaries who were not well paid and had poor chances for advancement (Smith 1979). Although the educational attainment of women has been increasing steadily and better education usually meant a higher income, in 1981 the salaries of women with four or more years of college was, on the average, $17,549, which was only 57 percent of average earnings of men with college degrees, while women who had graduated from high school earned, on the average, $12,023, which was 62 percent of the earnings of a man with the equivalent amount of education (U.S. Bureau of the Census, 1984).

The middle-class women holding better-paying positions have been given a good deal of visibility by the success stories written about them, but the impression that they had broken the earnings barrier in large numbers was a false one. Women still constituted a small proportion of people holding above-average and higher-level jobs. In 1981, of the women who were working at full-time, year-round jobs, only 5 percent or 1,170,000 had earnings of between $25,000 and $50,000, whereas 28.7 percent of the men or about 12 million earned this amount. In the $50,000-to-$75,000 bracket the proportion was one-tenth of 1 percent, or roughly 32,000 women; of those women making $75,000 or more, there were 21,000. In total, then, 5.2 percent of the female workers had salaries over $25,000, compared with 33.4 percent of the male workers (Women's Bureau 1984).

The employed women in our sample were, by and large, in above-average earning brackets—mostly college-educated upper-income thirty- to sixty-five-year-olds who thought of themselves as pursuing careers, not just working at jobs. A number of them, however, did clerical, sales, and service work, and therefore made less money and were not expecting to advance much in pay or status. Still most of the women in these non-career jobs were seriously dedicated to performing their duties well and expressed a high degree of commitment to their employers and bosses. A few owned their own businesses, while a sizable number worked part-time. For the professional woman or businesswoman who was a partner in a dual-income household, the combined earnings of the family were such that financial problems were not ordinarily an issue in how they conducted their social lives. Most of them, however, considered their financial contribution to the family income critical to maintaining their present life style. Those women who were heading households alone, particularly the single parents, were scratching to get by, even though they themselves earned salaries that were well above the average for female workers. These women felt considerably constrained in their social life by their limited resources, while at the same time they expressed the desire to join in more social activities with their friends and acquaintances. Their tight budgets allowed for few expenditures on their own recreation.

In most cases a woman employed outside the home held the equivalent of a second almost full-time job, which she performed before and after her paid work and on weekends (Epstein 1971). A working woman typically still organized the maintenance of her household and retained control over everything that happened there, or at least had the responsibility for planning and supervising the execution of the household tasks. Most frequently this meant she did the cleaning, shopping, cooking, washing, and all the other miscellaneous chores of housekeeping herself, that is, virtually the same household work she would do if she were homebound. She also attended the school meetings, participated in community activities, kept up the contact with the relatives, and sustained the religious obligations of the family. Sometimes family members pitched in, and the occasional woman had household help. Some of them employed cleaning women, live-in housekeepers, and nurses for babies and young children, but much more commonly she organized a patchwork of babysitters, after-school activities, and networks of emergency resources to provide for the care and safety of the children. Even in seemingly egalitarian marriages the wife did the basic planning for the household and assumed responsibility for day-to-day needs of the family members, while the husband "helped out" in limited ways (Pleck 1977, 1983). In only a few of the households had there been a significant reapportionment of the domestic tasks between husband and wife (Rapoport and Rapoport 1978, 1980).

Although differing in financial assets, the working women in the sample had one thing in common—an acute shortage of time and energy. Their supply of these commodities was frequently drained down to almost empty. "I am running on adrenalin," was an expression used by a staff member of a newly elected governor, "and something has to give. In my case it's my teenager who is suffering from my long hours and weekend work." As with most of the professional women we talked to, her allocation of time and energy were heavily tipped in the direction of work, and as with all these women who had family and home responsibilities, she felt harried and often guilty about shortchanging her daughter and non-work friends. But her duties required her to spend long hours at the office and bring work home at night and on weekends. Her colleagues on the staff were also putting in long hours and were under a great deal of pressure. "What all of us women need, " said a lawyer who was married and the mother of a two-year-old, "is a wife at home." But even if such women employed household help, that in itself did not take care of the shortage of time to devote to husband, children, and some cherished old friends. "If I could just have two more hours in a day, I think I could manage it." One common defense against feeling guilty about neglecting family members was stated by an executive secretary this way: "I am just counting on the quality of the time I spend with the kids to make up for what's missing in quantity. It's not really the number of hours I am at home with them but how we spend them. I really am so excited about going to work. I wouldn't give it up for anything."

Among some of the women there was a feeling that their coworkers did not sympathize with their efforts to be good mothers and wives while carrying on their work. Once these colleagues became parents, however, they appreciated the strains and pressures of trying to combine domestic and work responsibilities. In some cases women with young children at home expressed real ambivalence about the benefits of working: on the one hand they enjoyed the intellectual and emotional satisfactions that were provided, while at the same time they begrudged the time it took away from their families, friends, and other interests. Despite their heavy work and home responsibilities, most of the women said they derived a good deal of personal satisfaction from working outside the home and expected to spend the rest of their adult lives in the work force.

How did their "greedy occupations" (Handy 1978) influence the friendships of the business women and professional women? Among this group of women in the study sample, it was usual for them to have friendly relations with their coworkers, but less usual for them to refer to these colleagues as their close friends. There were some startling exceptions to this, but the professional and managerial women we interviewed almost always mentioned having sociable companions and acquaintances where they worked and among both men and women, but rarely an intimate friend. With the office being such a logical place to find friends, it seemed strange to discover that many of the working women did not become close friends with colleagues, at least not until they no longer worked together. There were a number of explanations for this. A woman who had risen to a well-paid middle-management position in a major corporation discussed the reasons she deliberately avoided becoming close friends with her office mates:

I have what I would call modified friendships with people at work because I believe there is a bare minimum that people at work should know about your home life. I really believe those should be kept separate. I believe in the separation of church and state. Why do I think that? For me it is part of my reaction to most people's idea that women are overly emotional. So I build some protection by not letting anyone at work know about my private life. That way nobody can attribute some behavior of mine to some sort of emotional problem they might think I am undergoing at home.

It's not that I don't socialize with some of them. I do know some of the women better than others—and some of the men for that matter—better than others, at least differently from others, but it certainly has not been a fast process and I've worked there more than ten years. I would say that a lot of them are acquaintances rather than friends. There are plenty of women at my level and above in this industry, so there would be a lot to choose from, but I don't consider it a good idea to get really close to anybody in the office.

Although it did not always hold true, the distance between the supervisor and the supervised was commented on as a deterrent to the growth of a friendship. Some bosses felt isolated by this and decried it; others took it for granted, believing that people of different rank have trouble mixing on a friendship basis. One woman stated it as an axiom in her work life:

I don't want to be friends with people who work for me or whom I work for. . . . I am becoming better friends with a girl named Sally; well, she's a woman of course, but she seems quite young, although she's only a year or so younger than I am. She used to work for me and that was the reason I didn't bother to get to know her too well.

I think Sally is very bright and has never in her entire life worked up to her expectations. Although I had always liked her as a person, there are obviously problems in dealing with a person who doesn't work up to her capabilities. When I would have to go over a review of her work with her and criticize her performance and have to say to her, like a kid, "Come on, Sally, what do you want me to do?" That's all gone now, since I am not her boss any more and we both report to different people. She is really great.

Another middle manager corroborated this view that it was unlikely she would bridge the gap between herself and the people she supervised. "It is hard for me to criticize an employee and then be friendly. I can't segregate my behavior. I can't be angry in a work situation and then go to lunch and to drinks and a movie. If I'm going to act at all businesslike, that is the way it's going to be throughout the relationship."

Some women said they made a practice of cultivating friends outside the company they worked for or in different divisions of the same firm. It took the reorganization of an office and the reassignment of some women to new offices for friendship to begin to blossom among a group of managers who had worked together for a least a half dozen years.

It was only when my department was broken up and sent us to three different locations that I realized how much I had really enjoyed coming in and saying hello to everybody in the morning and chatting. Now that they're a block away, literally in a different office building, I try to keep in touch with a couple of them. I had never lunched with them before, but we've started to have lunch every few weeks, just in the commissary. One of them, Robin, is getting to be a good friend. She can talk about anything, analyze what every one is doing. . . . She was in therapy for years and years. I expect her to listen to me bitch about Sandy not picking up her room too—that level of intimacy, and we joke about my bitching and she's—yeh. . . . I would consider her a friend. I am beginning to enjoy her a lot.

Most of the women considered the friendly interaction at work part of the attraction of being employed outside the home, even though the relationships were, for the most part, quite superficial and fleeting. In some instances, however, the women found that there was actually not a single individual among their coworkers in an office whom they could have befriended, even if they had wanted to. The women hired as token middle managers as a result of affirmative action, for example, found a number of problems awaiting them in how they would be allowed to associate with their male colleagues.[7] According to one such woman who had a job doing international planning for a major corporation, it was not even remotely possible for her to make anything beyond formal contact, not to speak of acquaintanceship and friendship, with the men in her part of the company.

I'm the only woman in my division and I've found the men, particularly the older men, are really impossible. You wouldn't believe what they do.

When we are in conference and I have finished making some kind of report, they say things to me like, "Well, you can expect something good from a smart Princeton co-ed." Their attitudes are quite incredible, but the funny thing is that they don't realize it.

So I really have no friends in the company, except for my secretary, who is a woman and is just fabulous. I keep my social life strictly separate, and luckily I have my old friends from my Princeton class who were recruited by a number of businesses and are in Manhattan offices—a lot of them in the major accounting firms, banking of various sorts, both women and men, mostly liberal arts majors like myself in English, history, biology, no connection with what we're doing now.

Anyway, I have made friends, new ones, in other companies, and they've all really helped me with advice about my work. The younger men are fine. No problems. It's just the older ones who have such outdated attitudes.

It was hard on her, she said, not to have anyone to talk with on a daily basis in an easy, informal way. It was a real drawback, she added, in her present position. It would have been devastating if she had not been traveling a good deal of the time. As it was, she was interviewing for another job and expecting to accept an offer in Manhattan, where, she said, the acceptance of women as ordinary human beings was further along than in the companies located on "these isolated suburban campuses."

Almost without exception the women in our sample who were employed as academics did not mention having any close friends in their own departments.[8] They talked about friends who were members of other university departments but not in their own. In trying to account for their friendship choices, they said they had just worked out that way, that the process had been a "natural" one in the sense that friendships, close ones, between people in the same department never seemed to work out. They had found that they were just more attached to outsiders. The decision about where it was most promising to make good friends had not been consciously planned or analyzed at the time.

Hindsight interpretations that evolved during the interviews touched on competition and jealousy between colleagues that might interfere with developing the openness and trust involved in a friendship. Department members, they said, were called on to evaluate one another for promotions in rank and for tenure.

Friendships probably did not flourish, some suggested, when friends were "in a position to be critical and judgmental about your work and your standing in the field, and have some life-and-death power over your career. I have a number of great friends, and they have all been supportive when the going was tough, but it seemed to work out better if we were in different disciplines." Although there have been advances in networking organizations among academic women and other professionals, these connections were not synonymous with personal friendship, even where they were useful as mutual supports (Kleiman 1980).

Loneliness at the Top

The women in the sample who had risen to top executive and management positions described what it entailed for their personal lives to work in this more rarefied atmosphere. At work they associated predominantly with other executives who were male and were isolated from peers of the same gender in their daily work environments (Linda Keller Brown 1981). In order to have reached this level they had learned to collaborate in a friendly way with the men who were their associates and with whom they seldom formed close friendships. Occasionally there was a senior executive who served as a friend, but women executives said they had to steer clear of friendships with male colleagues that might give the appearance of being a sexual one.[9]

As soon as a woman and a man were seen together at all regularly, even though they were conferring about business, there were rumors that they were having an affair. It seemed inevitable that most people would suspect there was a sexual component to a friendship between a man and a woman. "When Fred told me there was office gossip about our having lunch together and taking the same cab to meetings," a highly placed woman executive explained, "we decided we would have to conduct our business in our offices, even though it was less efficient and certainly less pleasant."

On the whole, the executive women were much less personally involved with their peers than the group of middle-level managers and professionals described earlier. In fact, for the majority of women holding high-level positions in business, government, and the professions, it appeared that personal friendship played much less of a role in their lives than for the women with work-centered friends or for the women who stayed at home. It was not that they did not have any friends or lacked social life; what they did lack was time to cultivate friends and keep in touch with the ones they already had in the fashion the women did in what we have called talking friendships. "I am not on my office telephone for twenty minutes at a time with women friends," explained an editor of a business publication, "and by the time I arrive home at night I am up to here with people. I've seen them all day long and we've kidded around and had some good times, but when I finally get home all I want to do is put my feet up and be by myself."

Most of the social life of these women was connected with business entertainment. The personal friendships these women had were usually formed on a couple basis. Because the arrangements for personal entertainment fell most heavily on the wife, she retained the veto power over whether the female partner in their perspective friendship couple was acceptable and what amount of socializing she could handle. Friendships, although rewarding, were also time-consuming, and many women found they were careful not to increase the overload by adding purely recreational activities with other couples very often.

Many successful businesswomen and professional women regretted that they had learned to avoid forming strong personal attachment of close friendship with their occupational peers and superiors of either gender. They stated, almost dogmatically, that they could not afford to be real friends with the people they were associated with on a daily basis year in and year out, the people with whom they shared the major portion of their waking hours. There were simply too many risks involved in trusting another person with damaging information about themselves. It was "unwise," "unpolitic," they said, to show anyone else the doubts, confusions, and fears they would normally tell an intimate friend. Most of them had support staff with whom they aired their management problems, and they felt "good about them" and thought they had grown "closer through tackling jobs together," but they did not count them among their intimates.

Although this kind of distancing from people seemed to be required in the conduct of American businesses and professions, it did not come easily to some women executives. However, they learned through trial and error what they had to do. By the time most of them had made it to the top, they knew intuitively how to protect themselves from the vagaries of personal relationships with colleagues. Consciously, or unconsciously, they steered clear of making bonds that might compromise their decision making or keep them from sustaining their positions or moving up the ladder.

The outcome of this for many women executives was loneliness disguised to outsiders by a busy social schedule and a rather extensive network of friendly associates. In a number of ways achieving women were becoming more like men in their social relationships. Although they had a wide circle of acquaintances, at the same time they had few, if any, current friends with whom they were on close and intimate terms. Many would say, as one woman did, "I really am too busy and involved in my work to worry about whether I am lonely or not, whether I have good friends or not." About such women it was unnecessary to ask the famous question from the *My Fair Lady* song "Why Can't a Woman Be More Like a Man?" For, in her friendships, she had already become "more like a man." Like many men, she had lost the easy "purposeless" relationships that have been called here the talking friendship. There was also the loss of relationships to the whole person; instead, friendships were conducted on a segmental basis. Segmental friendship involved being related to only a part of the other person—sometimes to just one activity the person engaged in. Relating in this partial fashion was typical of women who had good working friendships with coworkers and colleagues, respected one another's competence in that particular area, but kept their private and whole lives separate, even while deriving a lot of pleasure from one another's company.

Finally, like men, there was the loss by some of any intimate friendships, even outside of work. Although we know that many male executives and professionals have learned to live with only segmental, purposeful attachments outside the family, the question remains: Will women adopt the same patterns and be content with them? Some women, probably most top executives, have adopted the management styles of men or been chosen as executives by men who preferred women who played by their rules

(Linda Keller Brown 1981). But among the women in the study there were a few who had taken their need for fuller relationships to their work places and turned their offices into homelike places and coworkers into the equivalent of neighbors and friends. But putting down emotional roots into the work place was enormously risky on many counts. The equivalent of what happens at home, such as separation and divorce, also occurs during the course of any career. The women on the way up had been through those work divorces at least two or three times and realized that it made them vulnerable to the heartbreak of separation another time. They knew they would spend most of the hours of their days and days of their lives among people with whom they can ill afford to form bonds of close friendship.

However, a renewed yearning for personal friendship seemed to be rising out of the ashes of the work experience of professional and executive women. A renaissance of friendship among almost all the middle-class women we talked with appeared to be taking place. It was not so much that the women were discovering something new—the majority of women said that they had always had some warm and satisfying relations with women. The change lay in their rediscovery of the value of these friendships. The loss of the friendship bond was not an acceptable price to pay for full participation in this society. Depending on their individual circumstances, women saw their friends as necessary complements to an intact family or as substitutes for the traditional family unit. A pediatrician said she was trying to set aside time every week to spend an hour or so alone with a friend, almost invariably a women who had no connection with her job. An academic woman, starting her career as a promising political scientist, expressed it this way: "With so much change and transiency all around me, my friendships sort of make up the continuity of my life. I realize how much I depend on them for emotional support."

What seemed to be happening was a reconceptualization of the role of friendship and a growing recognition of its contribution to the well-being of American women in the 1980s. The women in the study expressed their desire to create some enduring attachments of friendship as a supplement or alternative to family and marital ties. In the following chapters they have told their experiences, good and bad, with cultivating and maintaining friendship ties, repairing the ruptures, and dealing with the numerous and complex problems characteristic of a close relationship.

NOTES

1. This phraseology had its roots in Jessie Bernard's argument that there is the "woman's marriage" as distinct from the "man's marriage." See *The Future of Marriage*, New York: World, 1972.

2. Our understanding of the contribution of trusted friends to the development of the self and identity came from the symbolic interactionists, beginning with Georg Simmel, Charles Horton Cooley, and George Herbert Mead and followed by Herbert Blumer, Everett Hughes, Ralph Turner, Erving Goffman, Anselm Strauss, George McCall, and others.

3. Some of the early studies of the formation of friendship focused on ecological factors rather than on the personal qualities and activities of friendship pairs. Whyte, for example, found that the people whose back doors opened on the same courtyard would predictably become friends. For the propinquity factor in friendship, see William H. Whyte, Jr., *The Organization Man*, New York: Simon and Schuster, 1956, pp. 365-386; Theodore M. Newcomb, *The Acquaintanceship Process*, New York: Holt, Rinehart and Winston, 1961; and Leon Festinger et al., *Social Pressures in Informal Groups*, New York: Harper and Brothers 1950, pp. 33-59.

4. We are reminded here of the notion that some social behavior may be best viewed as an end in itself, although, of course, talking friendships performed a multitude of functions, such as contributing to self-validation, role identity, and social support. See S. F. Secord and C. W. Backman, *Social Psychology*, New York: McGraw-Hill, 1964, and George J. McCall and J. L. Simmons, *Identities and Interactions*, New York: Free Press, 1966.

5. In his discussion of his own findings and a review of the literature on men's friendship, Robert R. Bell joined with others in finding that most friendships between men were largely centered around activities—doing things together. These friendships were rarely intimate and did not involve a major dimension of talking of the sort we found among women. Bell wrote: "I found in my interviews that often friendships with men exist both away from the job and away from home. Partly because many male relationships are based on doing things together, they must do them away from home." Robert R. Bell, *Worlds of Friendship*, Beverly Hills, CA: Sage, 1981, p. 88.

6. For essays and research on the stages in the development of relationships, see Steve Duck and Robin Gilmour, eds., *Personal Relationships 1: Studying Personal Relationships*, New York: Academic Press, 1981; *Personal*

Relationships 2: Developing Personal Relationships, New York: Academic Press, 1981.

7. In their classic study of successful businesswomen, Hennig and Jardim reported on twenty-five women whose careers started in the 1930s. They had long and close friendships with their bosses/mentors and with a number of their male clients, but not with the other men in the office. Few of them had any close relationships with men outside of work either until their mid-thirties, when they decided to take a breather in their careers, looked for husbands, were married, returned to work, and continued to advance in the executive ranks. Almost all these women had "only one or two close women friends, usually sisters or other relatives." Margaret Hennig and Anne Jardim, *The Managerial Woman*, New York: Pocket Books 1978.

8. Friendship and social support among women physicians in a hospital are discussed briefly by Judith Lorber, *Women Physicians*, New York: Tavistock, 1984, pp. 60-61.

9. For a detailed description of the interpersonal relations of women executives employed by U.S. corporations, see Rosabeth Moss Kanter, *Men and Women in the Corporation*, New York: Basic Books, 1977.

CHAPTER 4

The Extraordinary Relationship

> But with Deborah, I can tell her anything and have a degree of trust. But I would take it one step further: I can trust her in action. It really amounts to loyalty in the end. That's what it is. It's loyalty. We can count on each other being completely loyal. We don't expect each other to be perfect, but we know the other one will be loyal no matter what we say or do.

About this woman it could be said that her friends wrapped around her life in layers. There was one layer—the one occupied by her best friend—that was pulled close to the center of her life, and there were other layers of friends encircling her farther out. Like peeling an onion in reverse, she could tell you who was nearest to the core of her being, who occupied the next band, and so forth until she reached the outer skin. In her ranking of her friends by degree of closeness, she was not unusual. Less common was the deep level of "trust in action" and complete loyalty she felt she could count on from her closest friend. Although many women had friends with whom they aired personal problems and shared confidences, friendships of a deep level of intimacy occurred less often (Reisman 1981). When it happened we referred to it as "the extraordinary relationship."[1]

Asked to talk about their close friendships, a number of women began with descriptions of friendships started long ago. Some dug back into childhood and high school years; others referred to college days and early years of marriage. Even those women left behind for many years and seldom spoken to and almost never seen had remained friends in memory and were still thought of as among their best friends—"friends in escrow," as we called them. The investment in such friends had never been withdrawn; the friendships seemed to be banked for life. A number of childhood friends had never been out of touch with each other, sometimes in an unbroken span of many decades; others had renewed childhood ties at a reunion after long years of separation. A successful professional woman in her late fifties mused about a recent reunion with such a friend:

> It was wonderful being with Adele again. She lived across the road from me when we were on the farm, and we were best friends from grade school on up. Her husband was in our class or the one above, so I've known him that long too. Our paths have diverged. I went off to college and she didn't, but she developed her own talents and interests, so we hit it off very well. They invited one of their grown sons, who still lives in the area, to join us for dinner. I really felt as though I was part of the family, would even consider retiring there.

In their fifties and sixties many women expressed interest in reactivating especially cherished friendships that had been allowed to lie dormant in the busy years of middle adulthood. In their ruminations about friendship, they indicated in many ways a heightened longing for renewing their close ties to people outside the family circle (Weiss and Lowenthal 1975).

MY GIRLFRIENDS

For women in the United States, the pattern of having a special friend of the same gender starts early in life, but not at the outset.[2] During the toddler and early preschool years little girls do not show a preference for girls over boys as playmates (Maccoby and Jacklin 1974). They accept any child who puts in an appearance at the sandbox—at this stage the sex of a companion is not at issue. Any child, girl or boy, will do. But it is not long before all the children begin to recognize the difference between girls and boys as playmates, and by the time they are trotting off to kindergarten they show signs of being self-segregators by gender. In elementary school the girls associate predominantly with other little girls in their classrooms and on the playground—and they are self-segregators by grade in school too. At the same time the boys are turning almost exclusively to other boys for joining them in rough games, fighting, and forays away from home—explorations that the girls are forbidden to join. All the while this age and sex separation is encouraged by their parents, their teachers, and the rest of society.

Whatever it is that instigates early separation by sex, it occurs almost magically at the appointed time when the girls begin to appear in pairs, threesomes—and foursomes at the most—and the boys gather in larger groups with enough members to engage in team games on the playground and after school in someone's backyard. So besides the age and sex determinants of who will be whose friend, the number of friends regularly involved with is fewer by far for girls than for boys. Boys need more players to make up their teams but don't require much of their friends—only that they want to join in the game and have some skills at playing it (Lever 1976). In schools that mix working-class boys with middle-class boys, boys from both sides of the track will play together without knowing or caring about the differences in the family backgrounds, even though they might feel ill at ease if they visited each other's homes. By contrast, girls of elementary grade level would already notice social differences and be apt to stick with their own kind. Boys do not become deeply acquainted with their friends of childhood, and because of this their personal relationships begin on a markedly different basis from those of girls.

Already in the elementary school years the girls straggle home in small groups and play together in ways that encourage a much greater individual interaction than is required of team members. "A relatively consistent finding in the literature on the development of children's friendships is that boys tend to interact in groups, whereas girls generally maintain dyadic friendships" (McAdams 1984, 54). Little girls get rather well acquainted and can, if asked, describe a friend's characteristics and expected behavior much beyond the powers of boys of the same age, whose main comments about their friends center predominantly on sportsmanship and athletic ability (Bigelow and La Gaipa 1975). Although team members of equal ability are virtually interchangeable in boys' play, one girl cannot be a substitute for another merely because she can jump rope or play house as well as another. When making a friend, a girl makes judgments of many sorts about another girl's character traits and behavior. For instance, she observes whether another girl can be counted on to save her a seat on the school bus or wait on the steps to walk down the hall and into the classroom together. Her expectations are that a good friend can be depended on to do certain things. In addition, she begins to develop a sensitivity to how her own behavior affects the feelings of the other girls who are her friends.

In their choice of playmates, little girls demonstrate early tendencies to rate each other on a scale of desirability. Before they learn to disguise their feelings, they are remarkably open in expressing these preferences, and they can be cruel to those they consider the less desirable members of the group, say, to the child who is chubby and is taunted with a name like "Fatso" and put very low on the totem pole of friendship rankings. If a girl suffers from some other failing, like being bossy, she may never be able to win over a dependable friend, except somebody at the bottom of the barrel, like the overweight girl. So there is a rough sorting out of possible friendship pairs among the girls, using their own scales of preferred and disliked traits. Those of somewhat equivalent standing in the hierarchy are then candidates for mutual friendship, a process that also determines the array of potential friends throughout a woman's life.

As the pairs and threesomes and foursomes of girls are established, they become a kind of inner circle that develops a ritual and culture of its own. But its stability is never assured. In a foursome the girls are apt to pair off against each other. The threesome never works well for long (Simmel 1950). Sometimes the pairs are broken up by an outside competitor for the attention of one of the girls. If the interloper succeeds in attracting Nancy, Jane is heartbroken when Nancy deserts her and walks home from school with Carolyn. Tears flow. Sometimes adults try to intervene to re-establish a faltering friendship—to heal the hurt of betrayal. Usually this is to no avail. Often the girls make up spontaneously and all is well. In the battle for little-girl friends, the same inexorable rules apply as in love and war. Things may eventually settle down for awhile after a period of promiscuity and serial monogamy. But these early contests are for the emotional allegiance of the little girls, not the little boys, who might as well not be alive as far as the girls are concerned.

Clearly the course of the girlish friendship does not necessarily run smoothly, even for the times regarded later as days of innocence and freedom from emotional turmoil. There is a fallacy in thinking that an absence of pain in relationships provides a good foundation for the ones to follow. As in heterosexual love, it may be that friendship has only superficial meaning to a person unless it is cemented by some agony. Most little girls have, at some time, wept bitterly (and been inconsolable) when neglected and hurt by a girl she considered a friend. The fact that boys have not gone through this experience or are more immune to its effects draws attention to the differences in the development of the emotional life of women and men, seen particularly in the presence of the need for affiliation to a greater degree in women, and specifically with other women (Gilligan 1982; Miller 1976). These relationships are already of enormous consequence to little girls, as witnessed by their jockeying for position in picking off the most preferred child as a friend. There are great joys and satisfactions stemming from successful attempts to acquire a friend and carry on a friendship—and comparable pain and despair over not securing a little girl friend or losing one. A young girl already feels deeply about her connections with others of the same gender long before she reaches a level of self-awareness to comprehend much of her own psychological world.

But as they accumulate a few years of experience with friendship, preadolescent girls demonstrate that they have also learned some lessons from their previous experience with it. They look more to safeguarding their own security, partly through having a more realistic knowledge of how they themselves rank in the system and at what level they can successfully compete for friends among available girls (Douvan and Adelson 1966). By the time they enter their junior high school years, many girls form crowds that may last into high school and beyond. Dependability is key to membership in these groups. Within these cliques, girls may have individual friends who are especially close; these pairs are recognized by the group members as having a special relationship. Other girls never become crowd members. Instead they are likely to acquire a much more limited number of good friends. Some have a single friend or possibly an arrangement of making different friends in various settings, such as at school or church or in a special activity. The ultimate security posture is to have another girl belong exclusively to herself, someone referred to and treated possessively as "my best friend."

However, not having such a best friend during these years is not that unusual, and the girl who has few others she can rely on to run around with regularly can feel desperately lonely. Many indulge in fantasies about an idyllic relationship in which the two of them glide like princesses through all kinds of beautiful adventures together. The mystification of close and fulfilling friendship probably takes root at this period.

As much as it is desirable to have a real friend who can be counted on, the experience with this relationship that is so deeply coveted can also turn out to be immensely painful. When asked what qualities a friend should have, girls between the ages of fourteen and sixteen answered that, above all, a friend should be loyal and trustworthy, someone who provides emotional support when it is needed and, as proof of being a true friend, should never gossip behind your back—the cardinal sin of faithlessness. The following answer by a thirteen-year-old shows her despair over the inconstancy of her girlfriends: "I don't have many friends because people who call themselves your friends are really your enemies, sweet in front of your face and gossips behind your back. If you call those kind of people your friends, then I guess I have as many as anybody else, if not more. But it would be nice to have a real friend, one to tell all your problems to. All I have to tell my problems to is my diary" (Henry 1965, 151).

As girls enter puberty, the strain to be attractive to the opposite sex while at the same time being unsure of themselves with boys places heavy burdens on their friendships. What happens is that they divert the emotional energy of their sexual feelings into same-sex friendships (Douvan and Adelson 1966). Under such a heavy emotional load, these friendships can be unbelievably intense and at the same time prone to disruption because of jealousy, often over the issue of popularity with boys. A sixteen-year-old comments on the way competition for boys pits the girls against one another: "Another problem which I have is trying to get along with a certain bunch or clique of girls. . . . They are all cute and nice, but they are such terrible gossips I can't stand them. All girls gossip a little, but those girls carry it out to such a large extent, I felt I couldn't go out with someone new, and say anything about the date, without it going around the school very exaggerated" (Henry 1965, 152). Still the majority of adolescent girls keep on trying to find a bosom pal because they need to share all the mysteries of growing up with another girl going through the same transformation from girl to woman.

By the time girls have reached seventeen or eighteen, the intensity of their friendships with other girls declines markedly. A number of things happen to them. They begin to establish a clearer sense of their own identities. They are much more at ease with boys. In fact, at this age, for the first time, they mention the importance to them of sensitivity and mutual trust in the boys they go out with, somewhat similar to what they desired in their girlfriends when they were younger. With their friends who are girls, there is now less concern with issues of security and loyalty, although they still want a friend who is warm and understanding. But as girls become engrossed in courtship, they are less demanding of personal intimacy with their friends, somewhat more objective, even neutral, about one another. Still they need the satisfactions of the genuine interactions they had experienced with their same-sex friends. It takes time to make the shift from sharing confidences with friends of the same gender to sharing confidences with members of the opposite sex. Genuine friendships with members of the opposite sex may be limited by a reluctance to disclose real feelings and confidences. Consequently friends of the same sex are still preferred over those of the opposite sex throughout early and late adolescence and into the beginning of adulthood, even when young women's attachments to men begin to intensify and deepen (Jourard 1971).

Both one-on-one relationships with peers and friendships in groups and gangs become dramatically important to maturing young people as they try to disengage themselves from their families. Their ties with friends assume a dominant role in their attempts to establish a separate identity. Consider the following passage from Elizabeth Douvan and Joseph Adelson's work on the adolescent, quoted here because it is so perceptive about friendship and because in it these psychologists venture a comparison between adolescent and adult friendship:

> The peer relations of adolescence are part of the preparation for adult love and friendship: by loving and being loved, by making friends and being befriended, the child learns something of the vicissitudes of affection. We think he learns more than that. The particular advantage of the adolescent friendship is that it offers a climate for growth and self-knowledge that the family is not equipped to offer, and that very few persons can provide for themselves. Friendship engages, discharges, cultivates and transforms the most acute passions of the adolescent period, and so allows the youngster to confront and master them. Because it carries so much of the burden of adolescent growth, friendship acquires at this time a pertinence and intensity it has never had before nor (in many cases) will ever have again. (Douvan and Adelson 1966, 174)

Is it true, as in this suggestion by Douvan and Adelson, that there may be a peaking in friendship before adulthood—that friendship in the adolescent period "acquires . . . a pertinence and intensity it has never had before nor (in many cases) will ever have again?" This may very well be the case. Simmel is of two minds about this. He cautions against the expectation that friendship in adulthood can ever again reach the ideal of this earlier psychological intimacy.

> Modern man, possibly, has too much to hide to sustain a friendship in the ancient sense. Besides, except for their earliest years, personalities are perhaps too uniquely individualized to allow full reciprocity of understanding and receptivity. The modern way of feeling tends more heavily toward differentiated friendships, which cover only one side of the personality, without playing into other aspects of it. (Simmel 1950, 326)

"For most people," Simmel writes, it is sexual love that "opens the doors of the total personality more widely than does anything else. For not a few, in fact, love is the only form in which they can give their ego in its totality." On the other hand he also suggests that friendship may be more apt than sexual love "to connect a whole person with another person in its entirety; it may melt reserves more easily than love does—if not as stormily, yet on a larger scale and in a more enduring sequence." The special warmth that women feel and the fond remembrances they have about their childhood and adolescent friendships are well documented in the interviews for the Adult Friendship Project. But because we are only beginning to accumulate some knowledge about friendship in adulthood, it seems premature to make assertions that these subsequent relationships never have the pertinence and intensity of friendships in adolescence. We are only guessing. Nor do we know much about what Douvan and Adelson call the "pertinence of friendship for growth and self-knowledge" in the adult years. We simply cannot assume that the capacity for intimacy and reciprocity in friendship is no longer present in adulthood and that friends in mid-life and later years do not provide avenues for self-development. Indeed it is now taken for granted that as people mature, their interpersonal relations play a central role in their growth (Giele 1982).

"BEST FRIEND" IN ADULTHOOD

Americans are said to be open and sociable at a superficial level but uneasy about, even afraid of, intimacy (Hatfield 1984). This seemed to be true of the women who participated in the study, but they also expressed the hope that they would deepen the level of some of their friendships. The idea of having a truly close friend played an important part in the imaginations of many of the women. This perfect friend was thought of as possessing, above all, the traits of trustworthiness and unswerving loyalty and the ability to keep confidences. She was a person who was, at the same time, a good listener, an entertaining companion, someone with whom she could both gossip and air serious problems—marital troubles, housekeeping questions, decisions about childrearing and careers—a person to confide in comfortably. Ideally she would provide sympathy and opportunities for catharsis and self-insight along with distraction and fun. She would resemble the lifelong friend called a *shin-yu* by the Japanese. Between such friends "there are no barriers; one withholds nothing, and is never suspicious of another's motives" (Salamon 1977, 813). To go without such a friend made some of the women feel that there was something lacking in their lives, that they were deprived and were missing what they deserved to have. "What's wrong with me?" they wondered. They believed that they were the only ones to suffer the pain of not having a really close friend and were surprised to learn that many women never establish this kind of ideal relationship with another female during adulthood.

Indeed, close friendship was thought of as the quintessential relationship, the unfettered tie that was entered into and pursued voluntarily. To paraphrase the biblical premise about God's relationship with the believer, "in perfect love, there is no fear," it could be said about this human relationship, "in perfect friendship, there is no shackle." In other words, the ideal friendship was of their own making, undertaken and maintained without the interference of society. Insofar as it was shaped to their liking, it was a personal and private relationship between two persons who had exclusive control over it. This meant that it was beyond jural reach: no laws applied, no court actions could ensue from it. Although the folkways suggested some of its boundaries and rules, in the end it was the subjective judgments of the pair that determined the treatment friends afforded each other. In fact, it was the spontaneity of the attraction between two persons and the gradual delightful exploration of each other that recommended a close friendship so highly. The best part about it was that there were no set rules. In contrast with all the duties and obligations connected with immediate family and kinfolk, and the guilt produced when these burdens were not shouldered, friendship, they said, could be entered freely on their own terms, and it could be just as easily terminated if things turned sour or boredom set in.

But, at the same time, "in perfect freedom, there was uncertainty." In fact, the culture abhorred this uncertainty in friendship so much that people referred to friendship as an *institution* thus giving the nod of recognition to the existence of a social relationship without interfering any further in its regulation. What this amounted to, wrote anthropologist Robert Paine, was "a kind of institutionalized noninstitution" (Paine 1969, 514). In such an ill-defined "noninstitution," it was the province of the individual to define how the friendships of her own making were to be carried on and what was expected of these friends.

When we asked the women if they had a single best friend who was more special to them than any of the others—someone who also reciprocated this feeling—a great many of them named someone immediately.[3] But they also tended to back off from the assertion, not being sure either of their own selection or how they were regarded by the woman they had named best friend. It soon became evident that the interpretation of the meaning of the term "best friend" varied significantly among the women. Some used it merely as a way of ranking friends, that is, the best of the bunch. Others could not say that they would select one person as being a "better friend" than several other good friends, while another group felt they had never known anyone they would count as a best friend (Bell 1981). Moreover, there were ups and downs in every relationship; in addition, the need for closeness to another woman waxed and waned, thus affecting the strength of a tie at any one time. In other words, the mutuality of a shared relationship with a best friend had fluctuated over time (Chelune, Robison, and Kommor 1984). "I feel right now, " said Marjorie, "that I actually spend so little time with Arlene (the women lived in different cities) that it's not realistic to consider us as best friends in the way we used to be, say, in college."

The women were not quite sure whether a friend was close enough to be called a best friend. It was hard to know how the other woman really felt, since the stages of increasing intimacy were not always recognizable. Neither the length of the friendship nor the frequency of interaction necessarily indicated that the relationship had reached into the "central regions" of the person's being. Unlike a romantically involved woman and man who kept asking, "Do you really love me?" and "Why do you love me?" adult friends were loath to inquire about their friends' feelings for them. It would be uncouth to ask, "Are you really my friend?" or "May I call you my best friend?"

The middle-class women in the sample seemed to enter this unstructured realm of friendship with confidence about casual and "good enough" friendships, but a good deal of hesitancy, even wariness, about taking the next step to intimacy. There was uneasiness in talking about the urge to draw closer, and there certainly was discomfort set up between friends when they tried to talk about the quality of their relationship. Some women said that they told their friends they loved them—especially younger women

(Parlee 1979). Still, when face to face, the words sounded inappropriate. They resonated too much of the vocabulary of heterosexual love.

There was no equivalent of the engagement ring or the wedding invitation for a friendship that had advanced from being casual to being close, although exchanging gifts could be regarded as a sign of growing close. As the kind of gifts became more personalized, this indicated an appreciation of the friendship in a more objective way. Birthday and holiday gifts were seen by some as disguised pledges of a permanent commitment to a friend. In her essay on friends in *Among Women*, Louise Bernikow proposed the idea that gifts exchanged by women were metaphors in the "language of relations." Bernikow defined the meaning to her of such presents: "The glorious gift from Honor sits on my mantle—a leather-bound copy of my last book, marbled paper front and back, deep red covers. In this language, we offer each other double kinds of support—the body and the mind, the woman and the work, each part as valuable as the other" (Bernikow 1981, 115). Yet many friends would deny that gifts meant an acknowledgment of anything more than "what you would naturally do for a friend for her birthday or on Christmas." These were but ceremonial obligations expected of one's friends.

Although many women had made friends with whom they felt they could talk about their personal problems and feelings, it was much rarer for them to achieve their ideal of a "best friend" relationship. In their interviews some women said they had been disappointed in their quest for a fully reciprocated friendship. Their hopes for an ideal relationship proved to be unattainable. The resulting pattern of friendship was likely to be a cluster of several good woman friends with whom they shared different parts of their lives, and this distribution of attachments was usually accepted as a satisfactory arrangement. Thus it appeared to be more usual to keep some personal distance from others by means of including two or three friends in the nearest position rather than just one. In the process of winnowing out acquaintances from friends and good friends from better friends, many of the women simply avoided making the claim that they had a best friend. In some cases the women looked for their best friends in a relationship with female family members and/or with a spouse/lover. It was not uncommon for middle-class couples to turn to each other for much of the emotional sustenance and friendship they needed.

Of all the women in the sample, only a handful said, in so many words, "So-and-so is my best friend." Sometimes, though, when best friends were interviewed together, they seemed reluctant to admit that they were best friends in the presence of an outsider. Evidence of this came out in an interview with two young professional women from upper-middle-class families who were regarded by others as each other's best friend. After more than an hour of an animated session on the subject of friendship had taken place, Muffie and Barbara had managed to avoid discussing their own relationship, deftly sidestepping questions about it by bringing up peripheral topics, such as their earlier close friendships in college and the friendship aspects of their relationships with their lovers. There appeared to be no way of getting them to tackle the subject of the nature of their own relationship except to make a direct assault on their fortress of defenses. Hoping they would not squirm out of responding to an outright confrontation, the interviewer posed a series of questions: "Well, you two, do you ever say to each other that you are really best friends? Do you ever acknowledge that you are actually closest to each other?"

Turning with a questioning voice to Barbara, Muffie inquired of her, "Wouldn't you say it's not actually been said, but understood, right?" Barbara, looking at Muffie quizzically, replied, "Yes, but it's not *best friends* the way it was in seventh grade, when you talked about it all the time and you said, 'You are my best friend' and there was an exclusivity about it, but the fact it. . . . " (Interviewer: "Does it feel a little funny to have said it out loud now?") Muffie and Barbara, in unison: "Yeah, yeah," followed by nervous laughter.

Back on the topic of her other friends, Muffie described the recent changes in the number of friendships she had kept going. "I have kept in touch with my college friends and the girls from prep school, too, for years and years by writing and calling and visiting. I used to hold onto all my friends if I could. Now I'd say there are clearly just three. There's another Barbara and we spend quite a bit of time together. Then there's Susan—she's married and has children, a very busy life. She doesn't work, but there is a bond there, but we are less in cycle than Barbara and I. We have a different level of friendship. Still we are very close."

Turning to Barbara, the interviewer asked her whether she was jealous of Muffie's other friends. "No, no," Barbara replied, but Muffie chimed in, "As a matter of fact I *am* jealous. Barbara shares an office with another friend, a mutual friend. . . . I am not really jealous of their friendship, but of . . . I am envious, yes, it's not jealousy directed personally at a person, but I am envious that she gets to share an office with Barbara, but I don't feel supplanted by her."

But there was another recent intrusion into their friendship: Muffie had begun to live with Jerry, a man Barbara had introduced her to. Barbara herself had been living with John for two years—they had been graduate students together. The two couples were becoming a regular foursome. Barbara explained how this had affected the friendship between the women: "Muffie's being with Jerry so much changes the amount of time we spend together and also the pattern. Overall we spend less time together, but that's okay. If I need to talk to her, I just ask her if she can come up for a couple of hours and she always does so immediately or just as soon as she can."

Muffie, too, was in the throes of "trying to figure out how my being with Jerry is going to affect my relationships with other people. Does having a man in my life have to hurt my other relationships?" She drew some distinctions between what was happening to her friendship with Barbara, her acquaintances at work, and her family, all of whom had been affected by seeing much less of her:

> I probably worry less about Barbara because we live in the same building, so it is easier to see her often. My family just teases me about it. I am more concerned about my friends at work because I am spending almost no time at all with them after hours. With people like them, since I had spent less time with them to start with, cutting out that time drops it practically to zero. I feel especially sensitive and guilty about doing that to the women in the office who are not involved with men because I know that if I were in their shoes, I would feel threatened. That's why I have a rule to never break a date, say for dinner or the evening, with any

one of them, and I won't do that tonight, even though I want to very, very much.

Opening Up

In best friend relationships there was a gradual relaxation of vigilance over what the partners revealed about themselves to each other. This was a sign that they were on the road to becoming more than "just friends," when they felt less guarded about exposing the real person beneath the surface. Lisa and Rhoda were a case in point:

Lisa and I overlapped working in this office for one year. It was a horrendous year for both of us in our personal lives. Bad for her because she was going through a very difficult time with her marriage. Bad for me because my husband's seventeen-year-old daughter from a previous marriage came to live with us for a year. And I had welcomed the idea of her coming to live with us because I loved the thought of having a daughter, since I had two boys. I just thought it was going to be wonderful, but I hadn't bargained for a seventeen-year-old. It was an awful time. It could have ended breaking up the marriage. I used to dread going home. My stomach would knot up. It was a nightmare.

The give and take between the two women in working through their problems gradually led to openings for the development of emotional intimacy.

Well, Lisa and I were both going through these situations, and she still says she could not have made it through the year without me. I still remember. I used to love to come to work. We were probably very poor employees—we spent far too much time talking, drinking coffee, and crying on each other's shoulder, but being very supportive of each other. We were spending eight hours a day together, she and I, and I think I made her feel that she was okay and that I really cared about her. And she did the same for me. I think the approval was very important because we had doubts about ourselves and how we were acting at home.

Gaining this approval for their behavior in their stressful situations enabled them to see themselves in a positive light, despite their self-doubts. While Rhoda appreciated the support she received from

Lisa, she also expressed some discomfort about the possibility of becoming overly dependent on her:

> Every day there was a new episode in the saga. We were able to offer maybe a thoughtful suggestion or raise an issue: "Well, did he say that?" or "You must have been furious at that one." I'm not sure how much other people want you to need them, and Lisa and I have talked about that. Would we have ended up being so close if both our lives had been going great?

As they exchanged very private experiences, friends of this sort were conscious of some of the dangers involved. By sharing so much about their innermost selves, they exposed unattractive motives and behaviors of which they were ashamed (Hatfield 1984). But it was through the deepening and broadening of mutual acquaintanceship that they grew closer together. In the best-friend pairs the women tailored a unique relationship through the revelation of personal information about themselves. Dorothy put it this way:

> I think you have to have some sign from a friend that you do have something special. I think for a friendship to deepen and thrive you have to reveal a certain amount. You have to be willing to give more to a good friend of yourself than to just everybody else. It's not sufficient to say just that I admire her enormously or enjoy listening to her or that I respect her, it has to be something personal. Once in a very tense late-night situation when things in the office were in a crisis, Diane got up and threw her arms around me, which for her was an extraordinary act because she is a very non-touchy person. It was very revealing about her, not so much about how she felt about me, but that she was willing to let me see that she cared that much about something we were working on. She allowed me to see her commitment. That act was very important in the development of our friendship.

One of the critical elements in the development of close friendship between women in the sample was to overcome the fear of involvement. There was no doubt that the best-friend pairs had handed some of the control over their lives to each other, a daring act of mutual trust. This willingness to surrender some measure of power to another individual put both of them in a position of being dependent on the other partner. The resulting interdependency was predicated on the creation of a level of trust that gradually gave them confidence to increase their vulnerability. It allowed them to weather the missteps and faux pas in their friendship history in which they had both occasionally flunked the tests of sensitivity to each other's needs. "The growth of friendship," according to Peter Kelvin, "depends on, and progresses with, disclosures of areas of privacy. The disclosure of areas of privacy reveals the underlying causes and motives of the individual's behavior: this potentially gives those to whom they are disclosed power over him, and in doing so, disclosures make him vulnerable to exploitation. Related to this, disclosures of areas of privacy may also affect the individual's self-concept and thus . . . render him vulnerable to hurt" (Kelvin 1977, 367).

Clearly there were differences among the women in the study in the degree to which they were able to tolerate vulnerability. Possibly the individual capacity along this dimension may be a critical factor in differentiating individuals who were capable of close friendship from those who were not. There were women whose reserve made it almost impossible for them to break through the barriers to intimacy and overcome their fears of involvement. A young professional named Catherine talked about the hesitancy on the part of a coworker (whose friendship she had been trying to cultivate) to disclose any of her personal feelings to her or anyone else:

> You might think I'm pretty stand-offish when people presume to step across that line of friendly sociability to intimacy. But in comparison with Diane I am just a total blabbermouth about myself. She reveals virtually nothing about herself. She is one of these people with whom you have to be careful because you can feel the ice thickening. I can remember once when we were sitting and eating lunch outside and an ambulance went by. Without fail an ambulance makes me think of the night that my father died. That scene flashes through my mind and I mentioned it just briefly. I made some remark like, "Well, I guess I should have said something like that when I went to a psychiatrist."

Catherine realized immediately that she had made too personal a remark:

I said something like that and I could just feel her pulling away from me, and I said, "I'm sorry. I shouldn't have brought that up." And she said, "Yeah, I can't. I just can't . . . and why?" It wasn't for me to ask. I don't know whether she's had any psychiatrists herself, whether she wants to go and wouldn't go, I had no idea, but she telegraphs her withdrawal so clearly. Well, part of the reason she likes me, I guess, is that I pick up on that.

Ordinarily, this friendship would not have developed if Catherine had not persisted in getting the partner to open up, while at the same time honoring her need to hold back information about herself (Derlega and Chaikin 1977).

In the conduct of a close friendship, the partners learned to be sensitive to how far and how often the veil of privacy could be appropriately parted. It was a complex balancing of contradictory inclinations to be "open and honest with each other" and to be protective of each other's feelings. Although much of the research literature has emphasized the critical role of mutual disclosure of private thoughts in the development of intimacy (Jourard 1971; Altman and Taylor 1973), unchecked expressiveness between best friends could create problems (Rawlins 1983). Robin complained about her very good friend Eileen, who was placing burdens on their friendship by her lack of restraint in discussing her problems:

Robin: Eileen has been separated from Dick for two and a half years and still talks constantly about him. That's partly, I suppose, because she has a child and they have to be involved with making arrangements for Dick to pick her up. The fact is that without the marriage she doesn't feel like she's anybody, so she's in a constant state of anger with him. And I find it just so boring, it's just too long, too much now. So my feeling is that if she needs for whatever reason to stay angry with him, she should do it by herself.

Interviewer: There are some people in that situation who have nothing but problems, but as a friend you can feel overburdened with even legitimate problems.

Robin: Yes, I want to help her. I truly believe that she is a worthwhile person. I am tired of trying to get her to like herself. She has some responsibility towards herself. And she's also letting me down and that's become burdensome. At some point she has some responsibility to me as a close friend too. She comes to no conclusions about how to handle a problem no matter how long we talk about it. It's like every new problem is a new experience.

Interviewer: So it's not that she is revealing too much to you, but that she dwells on it constantly, that nothing else ever goes on when you're together. It's totally predictable what the conversations will be.

Robin: It's not that Eileen's revealing too much about herself. I am tired of talking to her about her problems and having every moment be traumatic.

In their relationships with their friends, it was not uncommon for women to try to fine tune what they revealed about themselves to even their oldest and most dependable friends, knowing that some aspects of themselves could not bear the scrutiny of others without eliciting critical responses. Francine du Plessix Gray expressed this in an aphorism: "All long-lived relationships depend for their longevity on a careful balancing of illusions" (Gray 1979, 4). Although friends were by no means always successful in hiding all their character faults from each other, it was possible for their relationship to survive such revelations, and even be strengthened in the process.

Elizabeth was going through the torments of the first year of a divorce that she had in fact tried to prevent. She realized she was telephoning her best friend too often and keeping her on the line too long crying and bewailing her fate, but she could not stop herself. In her calls, which were overflowing with venom for the man who was divorcing her, she knew she was exposing the darker side of her nature to her friend. Elizabeth's eyes teared up as she relived the many times she had not been able to resist blurting out accusations against Charlie, full of threats of violence.

I know from Regina's voice at the other end that she disapproves of those ugly emotions of mine, so I try not to allow myself to lose control too often when I'm talking with her. But lots of time I just can't hold back all my anger and hatred, and she's the only person I can express it to. Then I hang up the receiver and wonder what she's thinking of me for saying all those horrible thoughts and pestering her endlessly with my calls. It's not that I worry that speaking that way will destroy our friendship. I guess I regret doing it because I value her good opinion of me so much.

Elizabeth's image of herself was significantly tied to her friend's opinion of her, and although she considered Regina a completely dependable source of her self-esteem, she did not want to present herself in ways that would be in any way deleterious to the friendship (McCall and Simmons 1966). As a consequence she looked at her own behavior and tried to modify it so that she would not feel discredited in her friend's eyes. In withholding some aspect of herself from her friend's view—or at least shielding her from getting glimpses of some of "those ugly emotions"—Elizabeth tried to live up to the expectations of her closest friend. Many of those "horrible things" she blurted out to Regina she would never permit herself to disclose to anyone else. But she knew Regina so well that she was able to infer rather accurately how far she could go in exposing her innermost feelings to her. Because she was going through a traumatic divorce, she assumed that Regina would grant her a wide berth for the expression of the turmoil she was suffering and allow her to claim a disproportionate amount of Regina's time and understanding. This was an accurate assessment of Regina's response. As friends adapted to each other's behavior, with some mutual predictability developing over time, some extreme or "different" behavior could be tolerated without disrupting the relationship.

In Regina's case being a good friend verged on being cast in the role of a therapist. Whereas professionals have been trained to listen to other people's troubles and deal with their unacceptable feelings objectively, sometimes friends were too personally involved to be able to help each other endure serious stress.[4] "What is so upsetting to me," Regina said about the "horrible things" Elizabeth expressed to her, "is the depth of her hatred. She wishes Charles evil pain and suffering even after a year and a half have gone by. She is clearly in need of a support system. At the same time, by asking so much of me, it is impossible for me not to fail—which makes me a little angry. I want her to know that I am trying not to disappoint her. I know, though, that what's happening is that she is beginning not to trust me. Her distrust is spreading to everybody. I already know she feels she can't count on me." As the friend made valiant efforts to give as much support as she knew how, some anger and negative judgments about her friend inevitably crept in. But the crisis eventually passed, and the two women remained best friends.

Other women found that they could not respond to a friend's troubles to this degree, but still managed to navigate the rough stretches in their relationships. Bibi and Juanita had been best friends for almost twenty years during the time when their children were growing up. Juanita had a late baby, who, as a child, was always in some sort of difficulty at school or with his peers. Over the years it was to Bibi that Juanita often turned for advice about what to do with Anthony, and Bibi in turn tried to help out as best she could. But serious problems developed when Anthony reached adolescence; he was expelled from school for selling drugs and began to challenge his parents' authority on many matters. The police became involved; Juanita was distraught, could not eat, lost ten pounds in one week, and was on the telephone with Bibi every night at home and often tried to reach her at her office. Although Bibi was sympathetic with Juanita—she herself had a son with some school and behavior problems—she finally felt overwhelmed by her friend's need for someone on whom to unburden herself. After suggesting names of several psychiatrists to help with Anthony's behavior, she devised ways of avoiding these conversations with Juanita by having family members say she was out and her secretary tell her she was in conference. "I can't tell her directly not to call me, but she's driving me crazy. The more I talk with her, the more it seems to encourage her to call me. She actually seems to think I am interested in being kept au courant with Anthony's latest antics."

Although Bibi was ordinarily straightforward and outspoken in her dealings with others, she could not bring herself to speak frankly with her best friend because she could not bear to take the chance of hurting her. The silence about the issue was her way of bumbling through a rough period in their friendship and it worked out well. Juanita did not feel rejected because Bibi had already been extremely helpful. Acting on Bibi's recommendation that she consult a professional therapist, she transferred a good many of her problems to him and thereby lightened the load on Bibi, bringing the frequency of contact between them back to a more normal amount.

Studies of sociability and loneliness have indicated that people need two kinds of social relationships to ensure a sense of well-being (Weiss 1969, 1973). The first provides them with a sense of attachment that, for most people, comes from an intimate relationship with a spouse or a lover. For a relationship to provide intimacy there must be ready access, trust, freedom to express feelings freely, spontaneously, and without self-consciousness. Sometimes a woman establishes this kind of intimacy with a close friend, her mother, or a sister. Occasionally a man establishes this kind of intimacy with another man, although it is a rarer occurrence. The second kind of relationship provides a sense of community that comes from a network of friends who share our concerns and values.

If either a sense of attachment or a sense of community is absent, the result may be the loneliness of emotional isolation, an acutely stressful and restless state. Whichever one is missing, the only real cure is replacement. Even people with the best of intimate family ties may be intensely lonely if they lack friends, have few friends, or live in an uncongenial social environment. Married couples can be extremely lonely. And for the recently divorced or widowed, the attentions of their friends may be of help, but they will not prevent the loneliness unless they come to approximate the intimacy of the spousal tie that can occur in a best-friend relationship.

But friendships do not meet the needs ordinarily supplied by marriage, nor, by the same token, does marriage usually provide the needs ordinarily met by friendship. Relationships like marriage and friendship tend to be relatively specialized in the needs they answer, and as a result, people need both of them for their well-being. "If wholehearted commitment between friends is difficult—and this seems to be the case in adult American life—then it will be possible for friends to share interests, but extremely difficult for them to develop the level of trust which would permit emotional intimacy" (Weiss 1969, 38). In general, the data from the Women's Friendship Project supported this view. But it must be emphasized that not only were there clearly cases of close intimate friends in the sample—extraordinary relationships—but also a number of women expressed the wish for such a relationship. Those who indicated that they had very close or intimate friends went on to describe this relationship as one that was open and trusting and one in which they were vulnerable. On those occasions when a sense of mutual trust was reached beyond a shadow of a doubt, two women had no difficulty in saying, "She is my best friend."

Janet and Deborah had started such a relationship in college. Eighteen years later Janet felt safe in saying almost anything to Deborah:

> With Deborah, when I am particularly livid about something, when I am really going off the deep end about something at home or at work—which she knows I do periodically—I call her and describe how angry I am. I know that she can modify what I am saying in her own head and she's not going to go back to Howard (Janet's boyfriend) and say, "Janet said such and such." Well, I don't trust the others enough not to make that move. For instance, if my friends at work see me really angry one day and I make a lot of wild pronouncements about what I am going to do and three weeks later it turns out I haven't done them, then they are all going to think, "Well, what's her problem?" So in some way they are going to be judgmental.

As in the marital relationship, these extraordinary relationships between friends were not without ferment. There could be dangers to the survival of a friendship if one of the partners sought the possession, closeness, or commitment more characteristic of a marriage. Lacking close family or marital ties, some women occasionally expected too much of a friend. The demanding lonely friend wanted time, affection, understanding, and, especially, emotional intimacy with her best friend. When one of the partners attempted to move beyond the generally understood assumptions about the conduct of their relationships, the other resisted. Depending on the personalities involved, the women usually handled the tensions peaceably, but occasionally there were open clashes, precipitated by feelings of resentment, jealousy, and neglect.

With all the difficulties involved in developing very close friendship, still some women succeeded in maintaining a long-standing best-friend bond with another woman. Those who claimed to possess an intimate friend—an extraordinary relationship—expressed an almost childlike pleasure in the company of the other person. Friends of this sort knew that the other person enjoyed her for herself. "Anne believes that nobody else in the world thinks her stories are as funny as I do, or that anyone else is a better cook." "Jane thinks I am so smart because I can explain something about how the business operates that she can never figure out." "We can go shopping together and have the best time just fooling around." While best friends were not always so openly enthusiastic about each other, since they knew each other's faults too well, still the delight in each other had not burned out. There were special ties that held the extraordinary relationships together: shared experiences, loyalty, trust, enjoyment, and, especially, revealed intimacies.

Family Members as Best Friends

Some of the women said their best friend was some member of the family: either their husband, sister, or mother (Lopata 1975). Those reared in a working-class home had seen their mothers spend their time almost exclusively with the immediate family and the relatives. Their early social life had consisted of visiting with their own mothers, grandparents, married sisters and in-laws, married and unmarried adult daughters, with whom they found affection and acceptance, if not always peaceful relationships. A great many of the upwardly mobile daughters and granddaughters from this background had difficulty establishing ties of any great degree of intimacy with women who were not related to them by kinship ties.

Sisters as Best Friends

Elizabeth, for example, who had made her way from a Catholic coal mining town to a rather affluent New Jersey suburb by the route of a college degree, a promising career in industrial chemistry, and marriage to an accountant, tried to treat her neighbors as if they were family members back home:

> I've found that some of the friends I have made here or thought I had made have taken advantage of me. Like a woman who needed help when she was pregnant with her fifth child. I was glad to help out because I knew she needed someone to give her a hand so badly. I not only babysat but I cleaned her house for her—every week for at least two months. After the baby was born, guess what? I never heard from her again. I just don't do that anymore. There's a lot of turnover in our neighborhood, corporate transfers, purchases of larger houses. . . . But the moving makes you wary of making new friends, and I notice that the women who move in and are newcomers are cautious about it too.

After ten years of trying unsuccessfully to make a friend at the laboratory and then in the neighborhood, Elizabeth concluded that a relative was best at filling the bill.

> My sister is really my best friend. I could not really depend upon any of the other women I've known to help me make up my mind about keeping little Paul in public school as against parochial, which I don't believe in. I don't have any close friends with whom I would talk about things like that. My sister and I are very different, but she is the person I call up to talk about all the little things that come up with a child. Being unmarried, she is intensely interested in him and her other nieces and nephews. I realize that if she were married, she would be involved in her own family, possibly so much that we wouldn't be as close as we are. I realize I am very lucky to have her.

Sometimes, however, there were problems associated with turning to relatives for close friendship. The relationship between many sisters, for example, carried the residue of early competition for favored treatment by parents. The long history that was shared by siblings gave them common outlooks and loyalties but also included occasions of hurt, misunderstandings, quarrels, and jealousies. Current events could reawaken negative emotions related to the past. Nonkin friends did not come with such baggage, and although the relations between best friends could sometimes be difficult, the friendship was not saddled with the unresolved resentments that had developed between sisters. One woman whose sister lived some 3,000 miles away said, "You know, I love my sister and I guess she is sort of a friend, but every time we get together it seems like I get a sore throat and it's hard to talk." Still, in the sample of women, there were sisters who were best friends, particularly among the older women.

A variation of the tendency to confine intimacy to some female relative was the habit of trying to convert nonkin friends into family members. In these cases a friend of one member of a family was adopted as a fictive relative by the rest of the family and expected to play the part of aunt to the children and near-relative to the rest of the family and be present regularly at Sunday dinner and holiday gatherings. When this happened the attachment was so stable that everyone in the family circle assumed its permanence and treated the friend almost like a relative. The terminology of kinship was frequently applied to this individual, but with some accompanying awkwardness and ambivalence. The role of the family friend was usually ambiguous even though it was close:

> When my mother—she was born in Italy, you know—introduces my friend Bernice as my "best girl friend," we all lift an eyebrow at the terminology she uses. She'll never get over referring to grown women as girls. It's ridiculous, but I'll never change her. I'm fifty and Bernice is four years older than me, but I've given up trying to correct my mother. In a way it feels so good to have someone come right out and say in the open that Bernice and I are best friends. We never say that to each other, much less have anyone else refer to us that way. It's strange, isn't it? I really think of her more as a sister.

This first-generation Italian woman recognized how close her grown daughter was to her "girlfriend" and defined her that way with a good deal of certainty about the assignment of roles and obligations. Somewhere along the road leading from the city bungalow to the suburban ranch house, however, a great many of the second-generation daughters had lost that sure sense of how to define their close nonkin relationships. The problem for them lay in making the transition between giving primary allegiance to blood relatives and developing familylike bonds to women friends. It was the younger women in the study who had succeeded in freeing themselves enough from family bonds to develop non-kin close friendships.

Husbands and Lovers

Toward the end of the interview sessions, it was common for a woman to try to explain the reasons her husband or lover was "really my best friend." As one woman put it, she felt there was a difference in the kind of intimacy that could be achieved between two women and a woman and a man:

> There are things, I think, you can talk about with a woman because you know they've felt the same things, that men just can't feel. There are other things you can talk about better with men just *because* they haven't experienced it. But mainly it's because you can have a different kind of protective relationship than women can have with each other. And I mean

in both directions. There are ways in which he can nurture you on one day, and you can then nurture him on another day.

There's a physical dimension that is different. There are lots of taboos about physical relations between women that just aren't there with my men friends. We are free to have a physical relationship that is not possible for women who are best friends. You need that when you are really in distress. I can get that from a man a lot more easily than from a woman. It's not to say that I have never taken a woman in my arms, but it's not the same. You can only do that for a few minutes and then as soon as the worst is over you both separate.

The physical aspect of the relationships between heterosexual pairs was only one aspect of the relationship that increased intimacy. There was also a belief system about the emotional attachment that ought to exist between spouses in a good marriage. If the marriage was a good one, then it followed in her mind that spouses would be each other's best friend. If the relationship was not living up to that ideal, the partners should work on becoming better friends. Moreover, in their view, developing friendship in marriage was the supreme goal and more worthy of achieving and possibly harder to achieve than sexual satisfaction. A friendship of great depth with her husband/lover ranked close to the top of the various possible kinds of friendships she hoped to experience in her adult life.

Despite these fond hopes for deepening friendships with their men, many women did not believe that their husbands or lovers put as much of a premium on developing friendships with them as they did. The men were much more involved in careers than in their interpersonal relations in the marriage, even when a husband described a wife as "the most important person in my life" Bardwick 1974).

The woman who had not broadened her friendship ties beyond the person of her husband (or lover) appeared to be headed for some periods of loneliness as her family grew up and her husband became burdened with more responsibilities at work. Judith Birnbaum contrasted the lives of a sample of college-educated homemakers, married professionals with children, and single professional women and found that the homemakers were suffering from feelings of loneliness and isolation. In regard to the wife and mother who has concentrated on the personal relationships with her husband and children almost exclusively, Birnbaum predicted that the traditional homemaker would feel unhappy and depressed by the time she reached middle adulthood.

> Despite faithful devotion to home, husband, family, and community activities as central organizers of her life, she feels unattractive to men, and not especially competent at anything, even child-care and the social graces, let alone work and intellectual functioning. Having had plenty of friends through the school years, she now feels somewhat lonely and isolated. On the face of it, everything is fine and her life is moving along very much as she must have expected it to or even hoped it would. Her husband and children are described as busy and successful and rewarding to her. Yet personally she experiences an inexplicable sense of failure and disappointment. (Birnbaum 1975, 408-409)

Few women in the study fitted this picture of the traditional homemaker who had cut off all meaningul ties beyond her immediate family. Indeed most of them recognized the dangers inherent in relying solely on husband and children for emotional nourishment. Although the much heralded "togetherness" of the family-centered companionate couple held a lingering attractiveness, it was frequently pointed out that it was "unwise to expect marriage to provide everything." Even when a woman said she went to her husband first with her daily concerns and in times of serious distress, this did not preclude including others as reliable sources of support. In other words, the role of confidante was lodged in several trusted people—it did not rest *exclusively* with her husband. But the possession of one other best friend was also a rarity. Instead, close and trusted friends—more often several of them rather than only one—shared in the provision of nurturance. The women usually spread their attachment among several good friends, each one of whom had different abilities and special ways of satisfying her varied and complex relational needs. This division of labor lessened the intensity of the expectations and lowered the probability of disappointment (Jong-Gierveld).

Still a romantic conception of the perfect friend and confidante died hard in friendships, just as it did in marriage. The search for a total relationship was given up reluctantly. Some of the women were in the process of thinking about how they could respond in some creative ways to women's needs for a stable, nurturing, and protective relationship with each other. Possibly their overly exclusive reliance on men for the reciprocity of intimacy had been misplaced. It may have led them to cutting themselves off from anything but superficial connections with women. At least some of the middle-class women in the study had developed a complex and close relationship with their best friends who were women, and they expected these friendships to endure throughout the rest of their lives.

NOTES

1. On the importance of trust in friendship, Bell reported that "when we asked people to describe what was important to friendship, their most common answer was 'trust.' This was because close friendships are possible only if certain barriers are eliminated. . . . What they do and get from each other is based on trust. There is usually no questioning—no wondering about the other." Robert R. Bell, *Worlds of Friendship*, Beverly Hills, CA: Sage, 1981, p. 16. See also Elizabeth Douvan, "Interpersonal Relationships: Some Questions and Observations," in George Levinger and Harold L. Raush, eds., *Close Relationships*, Amherst, MA: University of Massachusetts Press, 1977; Irwin Altman and D. A. Taylor, *Social Penetration*, New York: Holt, Rinehart and Winston, 1973.

2. Evidence has been accumulating that children go through a series of stages in their relationships with other people. What the studies suggest is that children's ideas about friendship—their notions about what it consists of and how they feel about their friends—develop in a relatively orderly sequence of stages. These stages are roughly equivalent to the conceptions that children have about other people in general, including their thoughts and feelings about their parents and siblings—and the children's behavior is pretty consistent with the particular level of reasoning and insight they have reached. See Zick Rubin, *Children's Friendships*, Cambridge, MA: Harvard University Press 1980; Robert L. Selman, *The Growth of Interpersonal Understanding*, New York: Academic Press, 1980.

3. Lillian Rubin found that more than three-fourths of the single women between twenty-five and fifty-five whom she interviewed "had no problem in identifying a best friend, and almost always that person was a woman. Among those who had no one who fit the bill, only very few failed to speak spontaneously about how they regret not having someone to whom they felt close enough to say they were best friends" (*Just Friends*, New York: Harper and Row, 1985, p. 62).

4. Jessie Bernard suggested that one of the negative impacts of psychiatry was "its discouragement of talking to friends about personal problems." *The Female World*, New York: Free Press, 1981, p. 104. Criticizing the growing trend of using only "experts" for "therapeutic conversation," psychiatrist William Schofield called psychotherapy "the purchase of friendship." *Psychotherapy: The Purchase of Friendship*, Englewood, NJ: Prentice-Hall, 1964, p. 161.

CHAPTER 5

Breakdowns, Repairs, and Endings

> I really don't know what happened. I thought we were very good friends. . . . Before we actually went on this trip I noticed that something happened, something was strange . . . or it was just not terribly comfortable, and we tried. I said something about it to her and she wouldn't recognize that there was anything strange, so from that point on, I didn't know. . . . I would hear from her occasionally, but now I don't hear from her at all. So I will never know.

During the preliminary open-ended interviews about their experience with friendship, the women were given full rein to choose what they considered pertinent to talk about. There was a common—but possibly not surprising—omission in virtually all the accounts. They almost never mentioned either the deterioration of a once-valued friendship or the breakdown of a friendship that had ended in its complete dissolution. In this preference for dwelling on what had attracted them to their friends and the positive aspects of friendship, they paralleled the tendency of the research in interpersonal relations to emphasize the selection of acquaintances and the initial stages of friendship and to neglect those of growth, decline, and ending (Duck 1981c). While a number of women talked about their difficulties in establishing friendships and worried about their prospects in the future for finding friends among the women they were likely to meet, they did not bring up the topics of keeping their relationships in good repair and splitting up with old friends.

This silence in the preliminary interviews about the deterioration and dissolution of friendships alerted us to the need to pose some direct questions on this topic, if this stage of the friendship process were to be covered. It seemed particularly important to get some sense of whether losing a friend was such an uncommon occurrence that it was not a significant feature in the friendship experience of American women. In order to get some information about close friendships that had either lapsed into ordinary ones or ended, we were forced to ask some direct questions during the interviews. The questions were phrased in various ways, such as, "Have you had serious quarrels with your friends?" "Did you ever break up with a friend?" "Can you remember what caused the breakup?" "Can you remember how you felt about ending a friendship?"

When approached directly on the subject of the loss of friends, a number of the women recalled friendships that had ended and gave accounts of what had happened in some detail. In describing how they had reacted to breaking the tie with a friend, they frequently referred, in a matter-of-fact way, to dropping certain friends to whom they were only marginally attached and taking on new ones. Those relationships that were pleasant but shallow were easily discarded. Friendships of this sort had just lapsed. Other friendships that had once been quite close were brought to a gradual end by geographical separation. Some friends were lost during a personal crisis like divorce.[1] "We had a group of couples who saw each other almost every weekend for over ten years," said a woman who had been divorced for two years. "Then Andy left me and two of the couples became Andy's friends, not mine. They had him over to dinner and took his side. The other couple took my side and was faithful to me. Jeanette was really wonderful. I don't know what I would have done without her."

The turnover in a woman's group of friends was slow and usually not consciously planned. There was a winnowing process in which some friends might be upgraded and seen more often while others were downgraded and allowed to drift away. Only a few of the friends broke up in the course of quarreling. Most of the time the fabric of friendships in trouble simply thinned and then vanished. An unhappy falling-out of once truly close friends was the consequence of a number of conditions: among them were misunderstandings over sensitive issues, overintrusiveness into another's private world, the sense of being a hostage to the other's too intimate knowledge, and actual or perceived neglect and betrayals of trust. Feelings of friendship could turn from loving to liking very much, to just liking, to not liking, and sometimes to hatred—the gamut of emotions ranging from loving admiration to bitter vindictiveness. In intimate friendship, as in marriage, feelings of love and hate often existed side by side. "Because intimates care so much about one another, they have the power to elicit intense pain. . . . The dark side of love is jealousy, loneliness, depression, and anger" (Hatfield 1984, 209). There were terminations of friendships in which former friends went through intense emotional experiences similar to bereavement at the death of a family member.

It appeared there were both a number of conditions that were connected with endings and a variety of feelings accompanying these endings. It should be noted that relationships could be in trouble or "go sour" without ending as well as come to an end with some trauma. These two processes have been viewed somewhat separately in the literature, although they were intertwined in the women's accounts (Duck 1981c). On the one hand friendships in trouble drew attention to the constant need for maintenance and repair, the management of tensions, and the learning of restraints. The ending of a friendship, on the other hand, was different—involving more than failed management.

In general, of course, the extent of trauma in the breakup was related to the intimacy of the friendship—the depth of the emotional involvement. The loss of a truly close friend could be a traumatic experience. In contrast, superficial ties were severed and quickly forgotten. The women were not troubled by the termination of such relationships. They explained that their friendships had lapsed in the "natural course of events." They shed them easily and then went on to other friends. As common interests, activities, or a shared environment ceased to exist, the relationships came apart. The number of friendships that had petered out was a rough index of how many significant changes had occurred in an individual's life. When locales, jobs, and circumstances related to different stages of life were in flux, there was a turnover in the network of friends and associates to meet the new conditions.

There were two general kinds of responses to the ending of a friendship. One consisted of labeling the people who were no longer friends as having been only "casual" rather than "real" friends, and through this redefinition of the relationship, the women were able to discuss separation in objective terms and without much personal emotion. The second response consisted of recalling the experience in great detail and reliving the painful sequence of events almost as though it were occurring in the present. Both responses presented methodological problems in the study of breakdowns and endings of women's friendships. "As former partners struggle to reinterpret the end of their relationship, their view of the past will inevitably be altered. Our past is always changing as we gather new information on it, forget details or even major events, and perceive things from the new perspective of our constantly changing experience" (Johnson 1982, 70). The retrospective accounts of either declining involvement or serious troubles in a friendship that had led to its demise reflected the woman's personal reinterpretations of what had happened. They were not factually accurate portrayals of the events. The value of the stories lay in what they revealed about the significance of particular friendships and the general importance of friendship in the lives of the respondents—not in the validity of the reporting. While listening to women talk it was important to keep the distinction in mind between the actual *causes* of the decline and ending of a friendship and the *experiencing* of it.

FRIENDSHIPS REDEFINED

In the transition from mere acquaintanceship to friendship the potential partners had often made moves toward friendship of a tentative sort so that they could retreat quickly when they suspected they might be rebuffed (Kurth 1970). The hesitant steps taken in the beginning of a friendship allowed the women to look back on a broken relationship as if it had never been consummated as a friendship. Instead, the relationship was reconceptualized later in memory as a casual acquaintanceship in which there had been only superficial involvement. This saved face and protected the former friends' self-image. It also allowed them to avoid admitting either that they themselves had some responsibility for damaging the relationship or that they had felt slighted and hurt. The bond was redefined, and in so doing it was transformed from friendship back to a friendly relationship. Close friends could be shifted to other categories and labeled "just friends" (Jacobson 1975). In this manner of differentiating among the women occupying the inner circle of friendship, the endings were not regarded as "breakdowns." "You know, Cathy and I were pretty close at one point," Margaret said, "but we gradually drifted apart. We didn't ever quarrel about anything. I consider we're both mature women and past acting like kids. You know, we didn't call each other as often. As I think about it, I believe the feelings were mutual. Actually, when Jean moved into the neighborhood I found that she and I had more in common, and I could depend on her when I really needed a friend."

When looking for explanations for the change in the status of old friendships, the women were likely to seize on outside influences as both immediate and long-term causes of the changes in their relationships, although there did not appear to be a necessary connection between the actions of the "outsider" and the consequences that were reported. The effects of other people's behavior were interpreted by them as sufficient reason for the tapering off of a friendship. For example, the appearance of a rival for a friend's time was interpreted as the cause of a change in the quality of a friendship, although a decline in the attachment may have actually begun long before the arrival of the competition.

Redefinition of a friendship also took the form of questioning the assumptions on which the relationship had been based at the outset. Women would ask themselves questions such as "What did I ever see in her?" or "I had assumed we had pretty much the same values, but it turned out that I was wrong about that." A close friend of Wendy's had taken a full-time position in a law office. Suddenly there were empty spaces in Wendy's day that had formerly been filled with leisurely talk with Candice. Even when she met Candice for lunch she felt rushed because Candice had to get back to the office. Her evenings and weekends were different too, since her friend now spent most of her spare time doing housework, running errands, and just resting up from the pressures of her crowded schedule. Wendy was angry about the disruptions in the pattern of her daily life that were not of her own making. She tried to make some sense out of what was happening:

> I realize that Candice can't run her whole life for my benefit, but I see now that we really don't look at things the same way and I shouldn't put so much stock in our friendship. There were so many times over the years that we discussed what we believed about staying home with the kids until the last one was out of high school. Now Michael isn't even out of junior high and she's making him come home to an empty house. I just never imagined she would do that. I never would, even though we could really use the extra money, but I don't think it's worth if for the children's sake.

Not only had Candice's decision to take a job left Wendy high and dry, but it had begun to undermine the assumptions about the basic values that Wendy assumed they had shared. It constituted an implicit challenge to her own convictions about the importance of being home with the children, a central part of her sense of being a good mother. Candice had always affirmed her outlook on childrearing (Wright 1984). It was disappointing and confusing to have her friend let her down so blatantly by compromising their shared conviction that it was wrong to work outside the home when the children were still in school.

Of course much of the problem between these two friends did not stem so much from some new outlook on life as it did from the strains caused by having to adjust to the alterations in an established social routine. Wendy was going through the throes of reorganizing her day to accommodate to the shift in the amount of time Candice had available to devote to being with her. Depending on how much the relationship meant to each of them, they were going to try to preserve the friendship on a new basis by squeezing the friendship into the fewer available hours or they could downgrade the friendship by allowing it to taper off into one of much less importance than before the change. So far Wendy had not presented her case of feeling neglected to Candice and said she was unlikely to do so. She was beginning to worry about feeling estranged from her best friend, but she also reasoned that Candice had not been the wonderful person she had considered her to be. For Candice, it was her attributes as a worker, not as a mother, that needed affirmation, something Wendy was not in a position to supply.

A young newspaperwoman's account of what she called "my aborted friendship" illustrated the redefinition of a relationship once it no longer filled the needs of one of the partners:

There was this woman named Victoria who came onto the paper as the correspondence editor. She had worked at another publication before, a Bryn Mawr graduate, and rather large, you know, not particularly attractive. She had suffered a great deal from being overweight, I think. Not that she's ugly or anything. Anyway, I sort of became friends with her fairly early on. When I was first becoming friends with her I was just newly separated and considering a divorce. I was in pretty low spirits at that point. Anyway, when I left Phil and got a place on the West Side only a few blocks from hers, we became more involved with each other, doing things together. I was really rather lonely so if she asked me to do something, nine times out of ten, I would. She'd say, "Come over to dinner" or we'd go out to dinner. And since we'd take the same subway home after work, we'd say, "What are you doing tonight?" and we'd plan to go out and do something together that evening.

Emily and Vicki became constant companions and confided in each other a great deal. "It seems as if we both needed someone to talk to," said Emily. As time went on, Emily felt that Vicki was becoming increasingly possessive. "She bawled me out for not talking more to her when we were both at the same party. It probably sounds horrible, but I can remember being embarrassed about being linked with her in other people's minds." With these justifications for tapering off the relationship, Emily decided privately that she would stop seeing so much of Emily:

Gradually I began feeling more and more estranged from her. Then it got to be that I even preferred being alone to being with her. I began doing more things with other people, and I didn't feel I had to justify my actions to her. But by this time we had sort of built up a backlog of secrets and I guess I really resented that she knew all these little things about me. I just began to feel that she was so demanding. Towards the end she was having a terrible time with her boyfriend, so it was a relief when she left the paper and wasn't around the office any more. After all that time we had spent together she just more or less dropped out of my life, but I still feel funny about all those silly things I told her.

Emily had been able to escape from this friendship from which she had gradually begun to withdraw and had actually wished to dissolve sooner. As the benefits she initially derived from the relationship declined, she no loner felt committed to maintaining the bond.[2]

THE PAIN OF LOSS

Another kind of response to direct questioning about the endings of friendships contrasted sharply with the strategy of lessening the impact by redefining former close friends as "just friends," blaming outside influences, or discovering a friends's faults and inadequacies. When recalling the loss of an intimate friend, it was evident that a number of women had gone through "a really grueling experience" during the course of a breakup. There were two types of stories, both of which were accompanied by intense personal pain and bewilderment. One was a detailed reconstruction of the episodes leading up to the permanent dismemberment. "I was watching it take place and conscious that we were about to part ways." The second was a story of sudden ending of the friendship—of complete surprise at being cut off without warning. Both kinds of stories frequently pictured the friend as the instigator of the separation rather than attributing any of the fault to the narrator's own behavior. These women felt they had been victimized. In addition, they seemed not to have arrived at a satisfying explanation for what had happened. "You know," said a middle-aged businesswoman, "this is something I've never completely understood. I never knew what was going on in her mind because she never told me. It's sort of hard to describe. I can't put it into words because it was so intangible, but I could just feel she was pulling away. We didn't exactly have a falling-out, but it sort of ended. It was so painful to go through because I never really knew why it was happening."

Gradual Withdrawal

Although a woman may not have understood the reasons for her friend's behavior, she could usually recognize the indications of withdrawal. The changes might be subtle, but they were expressed in a special language of distancing: "I'm going to be pretty busy next week," rather than "Let's have lunch on Monday." Diplomatic illnesses caused cancellations of engagements. A friend forgot a special anniversary or event. "Suddenly you realize you're losing touch with each other. A woman I thought was a really good friend stopped keeping track of what was going on in my life. I was suddenly aware of this when she forgot the dates I was leaving on my dream trip to Paris, one I had been planning for months and talked to her about many times."

One clear sign of impending breakdown was a major alteration in the pattern of interaction that had become habitual between friends. Such a change in their usual way of talking together signaled impending trouble in Shana's friendship with Dory. "Dory and I had been close friends at college and then parted after graduation," Shana explained. "Just by some wonderful luck we both landed in Chicago six years later. I lived on the South Side near the university and she had a job on the north side of the city, but we made a point of meeting regularly somewhere once a week and calling in between. Then I met Tom and I am sure it was obvious to Dory that I was in love with him, but I still wanted to keep up the friendship and called her and visited her just as often." Then, according to Shana, things began to change.

> One thing she did—she wouldn't be alone with me. That was when I really knew something strange was going on. When I went up to her place—we continued to exchange visits—there was always somebody else there. There would be another person, say, someone from work, not anyone she knew particularly well, but somebody serving as a buffer between us, so that we couldn't have a serious conversation. I could tell that she was pulling out. I remember coming home on the el, crying all the way.

It was during the summer that Dory took the final steps to cut off the friendship. "When Tom left town for the summer, Dory agreed to let him park his car on the street in front of her house because it was safer there than at my place. All she had to do was to move it once a week from one side of the street to the other for the street cleaners." As a psychologist, Shana recognized what Dory's subsequent actions probably meant: "One day when she was moving the car, she hit three cars and a tree and totaled the car. The car was an old rattletrap, so it was no big deal, but she didn't level with me about how it had happened. There was some lumber in the car that she salvaged. I can remember that it became a big issue about how to get it from her home to my place." It was becoming apparent, Shana pointed out, that Dory was aiming for complete withdrawal.

> She went through this elaborate contrivance to make arrangements that would keep us from meeting, to be sure she didn't have to come into face-to-face contact with me. She created this fiction that a friend of hers was coming to my neighborhood on some other business and it would be easy for him to drop the boards off on the way. Of course I could see through that. It was so transparent that he was making a special trip to deliver the lumber.

This appeared to be the final breaking off. "I can remember as though it was yesterday when this guy dumped those two by fours on the floor-that act in itself was the end of me and Dory. It gave me the clear mandate not to call her, and I never spoke to her again. It hurt me so much it was several years before I could try to get close to another woman." The rupture, Shana thought, was caused by Dory's wish for an exclusive relationship. She felt jealous of Tom, whom she resented for ousting her from first place in Shana's life. "She didn't ever say she felt betrayed, but she acted like a jilted lover. It wasn't good enough for me to be close friends. I think she felt supplanted by Tom. It had to be all or nothing."

Sudden Endings

There were some stories of the sharp cutoff of a friendship—a "sudden death." Frances Ann, a handsome, beautifully dressed businesswoman in her late fifties, ruminated about the mysterious collapse of a friendship made during her first pregnancy, more than thirty years earlier. She was still trying to figure out what had gone wrong: "I brought her a house gift, which wasn't much—I couldn't afford much—and then just all of a sudden, they just stopped seeing us. . . . I ran into her husband a couple of times, and he was very noncommittal, just very casual and I never did figure it out." But Frances Ann continued to try to make sense of the situation. "Why? and I've wondered, many times since. Was it because I didn't give her a more lavish gift considering all she had given to me for Peggy when she was born? But I had talked to other people about her and, ah, they had had the same thing happen to them, that the friendship suddenly ceased, without knowing why. I never did know why. . . . I called, yes I called." The interviewer asked, "Did you try to get together?" She nodded and replied, "Yes," almost on the verge of tears. Then the interviewer inquired, "And what was her response?" She replied softly, "Having other things to do. So as, in the case of all rejection, you know, you just stop." Then the interviewer said, "That must have been very difficult." "It was," she replied. "We had been so close. She really meant an awful lot to me."

There were several cases in which malevolent interference by others was assumed to be at work. Louise, a prosperous businesswoman in her late forties, still felt the pain of having her closest friend bring their relationship to an abrupt ending. "Marliss and I became fast friends when we moved to this area nineteen years ago. We pushed baby carriages together, though we were not neighbors, so that took a little doing. We had so many things in common that we liked to do together. We took all kinds of classes together. She was a very interesting person and I was very, very fond of her. We also belonged to the same woman's organization." Then, "out of the blue," Marliss proposed that they temporarily discontinue the relationship.

I don't know exactly what happened or why it happened, but one day she called me up and said, "We have got to stop this Bobbsey twins relationship," and I said, "What do you mean?" She said, "We are seeing far too much of one another," and . . . then I said, "I don't understand what you're talking about. I really don't understand what you are trying to say to me." Then she said to me, "Well, I think we should not see or speak to one another for awhile." And I could scarcely speak but I said something like, "That's all right with me."

The women reacted to such sudden endings with surprise and then anger, and always with great pain. Louise described her feelings:

> I was hurt, I was really and truly hurt. We were very close, yes, very, very close, and I could not believe it. Up until this very day I really do not understand it. I tried very hard to sort through the things that had happened, that could have brought that on. I didn't talk to anybody else about it except my husband and he said to forget it, to just leave it alone. But it was very awkward because we were included socially in the same groups. At parties I would nod to her but I never approached her, never, never, but I missed her.

In working through the pain of separation Louise came to feel that outside influences had played an important part in the ending of this friendship. "I think there were other people involved in saying something like, 'Oh, you two are the Bobbsey twins.' I have always felt there was a third party involved in the thing, but she has never offered an explanation, and I have never inquired." It appeared that the hurt Louise felt was tempered by her interpretation that there was a malicious interloper—"a third party involved in the thing."

There were no instances in which the sudden cut-off of the relationship was seen as based on a mutual decision. Instead, one of the partners was left behind, often bewildered, "without knowing why." The friendship remained unfinished, with the abandoned partner speculating, sometimes for years afterward, about what had happened. A few of the women remembered taking the initiative themselves to put an abrupt end to a friendship. A prominent leader in civic affairs recalled how angry she had been with a longtime friend:

> I don't know how I could have been so stupid. She was just using me for social climbing and at the same time gossiping behind my back. I really believe she is an evil person. When I heard what she had said about my children, I refused to take her telephone calls. I told everyone in the family to tell her I was out and I simply said something to the effect "I'm too busy to talk" if I happened to answer her call. She finally caught on and stopped calling.

The discarded friend had never understood why she had been dropped, and she tried for years to discover the reason she was rejected by her friend, who continued to hear about her through mutual friends: "People tell me even now that she still keeps asking everyone we know what happened to our friendship. Some have reported that she even cries about it. Lord, this happened years ago. She is such a manipulative woman. What I don't understand is myself. How could I have not seen what she was really like? I was so stupid." But she had never confronted her friend directly with her grievances.

Many of the women involved in the breakup of a close friendship had not "worked through" their emotional reactions to their wounds. They had only partly laid to rest the sadness, diminished self-esteem, and even bitterness associated with the loss. More often than not, they were still addressing some old questions that continued to haunt them: "Why did it happen to me?" "Why didn't she tell me what went wrong?" "What did I do?" "Why didn't we talk about it?" In their postmortems these questions were still unanswered. They were still groping for the answers. Their stories did not provide them with adequate justification or a final explanation for their friend's withdrawal. On the contrary, they seemed to be once again retracing the events of the breakdown to make some sense of it to themselves. In many cases the breakup remained an enigma, one that they had been unable to resolve and put behind them.

MAKING REPAIRS

Some of the women seemed to be able to air their complaints and settle differences with their friends without harming the relationship. This group was exceptional in their capacities to repair serious strains in their friendships. Jean, who managed a research institute, had learned ways of getting over her initial anger with her neighbor-friend by telling her immediately that she felt upset with her:

> I have always told Peg right away what bothered me, usually small stuff. But I have quarreled with her and felt very upset with her. But she and I have always made up. She is one of the few people I can do that with. I

have a much harder time making up with my husband, much harder, but maybe that's because that's much more emotionally loaded.

Jean recalled a particularly serious falling out that she had with Peg, one that had come close to resulting in a breakup between them.

I remember that time we did have a pretty bad quarrel over money. It took longer to settle than most of the other things. I told her I was really angry with her, and we both thought the other was being unreasonable. It lasted quite a while, but we never stopped speaking. She lives across the street and we would always say "hello." But I felt a lot less close.

I would say to my husband, "If she's going to act like that, I am going to start being difficult too." Hell, you know, a lot of that kind of thing was going on. There was continuing resentment about it. We didn't really tell each other all of our feelings, some of them, but not all of them. The one thing was that we didn't ever *not* speak. After a whole lot of negotiations, we agreed to split it down the middle, which I thought was fair. After that there was still a strain, but that eventually died away. The strain has disappeared now.

Other women said that even when they were disturbed by something substantially upsetting about a friend's behavior, they thought long and hard before broaching the subject. Women who were good friends seldom expressed open disapproval of each other for fear of hurting feelings and permanently harming the relationship. Having so little experience with raising objections to a friend's conduct, they were not especially skilled at doing it. A young professional explained that she knew she was going to "get an incredible amount of hostility and defensiveness back" when she took a friend to task for how she was behaving:

We all were extremely upset with Jessie. She was recently separated from her husband and was sort of running after men. That was understandable, but she was doing it at our parties, just throwing herself at men and I mean literally. It was driving us all around the bend, and I won the lottery to be the spokesperson to tell her that her behavior was simply unacceptable. That was not my luckiest day.

It was unbelievably painful for me to do. She was extremely angry with me and also upset. Over the next several months we discussed it back and forth heatedly. She said I shouldn't have started off by telling her her sins, that I should have started off by expressing my concern for her because by the time I got to my concern over her, she knew I was really angry and she was angry back at me. It was painful to me because I thought her behavior was really bad, and I didn't think she was sufficiently contrite.

We have discussed it so many times since then. I think I've learned from the experience how I would approach a friend whose behavior I consider unacceptable. I wouldn't do it as brusquely. I don't know though if I would ever do it again.

A strong commitment to their ideals of friendship—and the value of friendship bond in their lives—underlay the efforts of some of the women to understand the dynamics of the relationship. Annie said, "It's quite hard to let go of old friends. . . . It's against my nature to give up the old. At least I'd like to understand why it's happening." Annie and Jill had become friends at boarding school, and although they were separated when they attended different colleges, they had written, made telephone calls, and kept up with how their careers were developing, Annie on the East Coast, Jill on the West. Finally, Jill came to Boston for a three-day reunion that had been planned for many years. It was during a period when Annie was having migraine headaches, and she developed a severe one on that weekend. As Annie put it, "Jill was totally impatient with me. Here she had come 3,000 miles and wanted to have a good time. I can understand how she felt. Anyway, after she went back, I never heard from her again." Annie compared Jill's unfeeling response to her illness with the help she had received from new friends and even from semi-strangers at her office:

At the time I felt very bitter. I really felt abandoned. God damn it, I have people around me who have hung in there. They would do things like come over and spend the night, really things I will never forget, and this group of women have been through months and months of ups and downs with me. I needed a lot of support. Sometimes I could get it from them and sometimes I couldn't, but they didn't have this long history I had with Jill that I thought made us so solid and sure. For a while it threatened my perspective on old friends. It was kind of destructive of my view of them.

After a silence of about two years, Annie received a Christmas card from Jill with "a very sort of chatty note on it, how are you, let's catch up and stuff." Although Annie had not responded to Jill's renewal of contact, she was speculating about whether she might get in touch with Jill on an upcoming business trip to San Francisco: "Now that I am feeling much better, I have a lot more perspective. I feel more saddened than bitter, and I think that's what moves me to try to settle it somehow." She had thought through how she would approach Jill: "I think I would call ahead and say I would like to see her, but for me it can't be just superficial chatter. I would say that I would come to the meeting with the expectation that we would talk about what happened. I feel that getting together and chatting and pretending it never happened would be totally inappropriate. I would give her the choice." If the reunion was to take place, Anne thought it should be a time to talk openly about some of the problems in their relationship:

I was thinking through what I would want to have come out of it. One of the things that came out during that visit was that there was really great competitiveness between us. She is someone who went to the Coast from the East to get away from a lot of Waspy, proscriptive stuff she'd grown up with. Everything was living in the East versus not living in the East. She was so uptight about it. I told her that I am just living here, you know. I am not declaring geographic allegiance every day of my life.

Annie was hoping to come to terms with some issues in friendship that went beyond this individual relationship:

I don't like leaving parts of my past out there unresolved. For the past few years there have been more relationships that have ended like that—unclearly. I feel very mixed. I feel that this relationship wasn't what I thought it was, but it is quite hard to let go of old friends. I've discovered that I like the quality of the relationships with people in my adult life better than those that began when I was much younger, but it's against my nature to give up the old. At least I'd like to understand why it's happening.

Making Up Was Hard to Do

The descriptions of breakups of friendships by the women in the sample indicated that the really serious ruptures were seldom mended. "Suddenly, Harriet had no time for me," Sandra recalled bitterly. "She was always putting me on hold when I telephoned her. She broke lunch dates at the last minute. I couldn't get her to commit herself to any engagement, even a month ahead. Finally, after a couple of months—maybe it was four or five weeks—I decided to ask her whether I had done something to offend her. She just said, 'Oh, absolutely not' and changed the subject. I simply stopped calling her and we drifted apart."

About a year later the two women met at a professional meeting, where Harriet took Sandra aside and told her that she was just coming out of a bad period psychologically and that her coolness had been nothing personal. Could they take up where they left off? Although they went through the motions of talking on the telephone and meeting for lunch once again, Sandra found the connection between them had been damaged beyond repair. "That kind of magical bond between friends had snapped, at least on my part. I'm afraid I just couldn't trust her not to cut me off again."

Once the fabric of a friendship had been badly torn, it was almost impossible to weave it back together again. Trust, it appeared, was the key element in any close friendship: when one of the friends felt that she had been unaccountably neglected or that her confidence had been betrayed, there was little likelihood that the friendship could be patched up, especially if an attempt at reconciliation was delayed. The women expected their friends to "behave properly" when, for example, they were called on for sympathy or help in an emergency. Faithfulness in carrying out such obligations was critical to the maintenance of a relationship. Lapses in honoring the unwritten code of friendship to respond appropriately in times of distress caused serious strains. Tamara was on the verge of tears as she gave an account of being let down by her friend Shirley:

My friendship with Shirley, my girlfriend from Atlanta—we grew up together and we've known each other's families all these years—will probably not survive. In April my father was in a serious car accident. At first it seemed to involve just cuts on his forehead, a bruised rib cage, and a broken leg, but several weeks later they discovered a tear in a heart valve and blood clots in his lungs. I called Shirley to tell her because she is my only friend up here who knows my father. She was supportive on the phone, but she never called me back to ask how he was doing. I must say that hurt. I don't care how busy someone is, a friend can take three minutes and call to ask about someone's health. I cannot bring myself to call her about this. I am too upset about the situation. I have not seen or spoken to her since before Memorial Day, I do not intend to call her. I don't know what I would say.

We earlier noted the sudden ending of the friendship between Louise and Marliss. This friendship, however, did provide one of the few examples of the renewal of a friendship after a major break. But this friendship, too, never regained the same level of trust and intimacy. Louise described the reconciliation with Marliss: "About two years passed and one day I got a phone call from her. She said to me that she felt very badly about what she had said, that she was sincerely sorry, and could we begin afresh?" Louise was taken aback by this proposal, particularly since Marliss did not offer any kind of explanation for what she had done. Louise told her that she would have to give some thought to the idea because she did not want to be hurt like that again. "I did not want to be party to that weird behavior." Marliss telephoned Louise several times before getting her to agree to resuming the relationship and the friendship proceeded on a formal basis for several years:

If we saw each other at a party, we would visit with each other for awhile. Actually what brought the whole thing back to where we really started to become friends again was when her husband's father passed away. We had gone to Europe on the day of his death and some one called to tell me about Mark's father's death, so I sat down in our hotel room and wrote them a note—purely a note of condolence on a courtesy level. I wasn't even thinking in terms of a rapprochement. I was just thinking in terms of acknowledging someone's hurt. But when we came back they were so touched and that was when our friendship resumed all over again.

Although the friendship was renewed, it never again reached the same level of closeness. "Today we have a very good relationship. She has had some very severe parent problems and she has called and we have talked about them. We do not necessarily have a conversation every week, but sometimes it's twice a week that she'll call or I'll call her, because in the back of my mind I have always held back." Marliss was unable to believe that Louise could be a trustworthy friend again: "Years later it hurts as much now just thinking about it. We have a very nice relationship, but it is certainly not at the same depth and level as before. I felt as if I could not resume it after those years I had been put in an incredibly uncomfortable situation with so many friends in common and we would see them all the time and not be on speaking terms."

FRIENDSHIP: THE PEACEABLE RELATIONSHIP

When two persons have learned to count on each other as reliable sources of positive response to many parts of themselves, they tried to act in ways that would assure the continuance of the tie (Turner 1970). It was common for them to overlook the qualities and behavior of the other person that could undermine their good opinions of each other. They tended to make many allowances for their frailties and weaknesses—even the annoying habits, referring to them, if at all, in endearing terms. They were unrealistic, to a large extent, where their friends were concerned and continued to think the best of them despite much contrary evidence. This kind of tolerance was a hallmark of devoted friends.

In most cases when tensions crept in, friends had ways of handling them without putting the relationship in jeopardy. One tactic was to ignore the problem in hopes it was temporary. Another was to treat it with a light touch. "Oh, come on, June, cut that out. You're just feeling sorry for yourself." Women were good at humoring each other with gentle scolding and joking. However, personal habits that were ordinarily overlooked could turn into sources of real irritation. "I have a friend," said Anne, "who throws in the expression 'you know' about every other word as she talks. That's probably an exaggeration, but once I noticed it, I began waiting for her to say it instead of listening to what she was saying. It really got to me." Still, Anne explained, she had never found a tactful way of bringing it to her friend's attention, so she decided she would force herself to ignore it. Complaining about it to other friends, she added, helped to get it out of her system. Between most friends, there was a kind of conspiracy of good cheer.

Most of the middle-class women in the study were simply too well mannered to bring unpleasant feelings of jealousy, resentment over neglect, and disapproval of certain actions to the surface. "It would just cause a row, and I certainly don't want that to happen. I don't have friends to quarrel with." It was unusual for a woman to claim, as Ruth did, that "I think maybe sometimes you have friends to have fights with. I've had a few rows with Julia. We are both very explosive people. Having a friend you have to be polite with, I think, puts the friendship on another level, takes some of the nitty-gritty, some of the meat, out of it." For the most part, however, the friendships of the women in the study were lacking in this sharp-edged quality. It was a peaceable relationship. The women went to each other for support and understanding, not for acrimonious discussion and petty criticism. Even when they exchanged ideas and differed strongly in their opinions, their tongues were civil. The longer and better you knew a friend, they said, the more conscious you were of your friend's sensitivities and vulnerabilities. There were topics to be skirted around and others to be avoided. In addition, friends stayed out of each other's way when tensions surfaced between them. Irritations were decreased when they were not inflamed by daily contact. "Even though I like her so much, there are times when it works better if we don't see much of each other."

Friends wanted their friends to be biased in their favor. They were expected to build up each other's morale, not tear it down. Although women said they asked each other for advice, they actually did not want their friends either to be critical of them or to recommend some radical basic alteration in their behavior, but rather to serve as sounding boards. When judgments were offered they were usually tempered by modest suggestions for change, not recommendations for the repair of real flaws. Friends were used to test out reality on the one hand while softening its impact on the other.

Although women described their friends in positive and often glowing terms, they were not blind to their weaknesses. When they made critical remarks about their friends to others for being self-centered, inconsiderate, immature, burdensome, even dull and boring, it did not mean that they intended to discontinue the relationship and give up the valued part of the bond. Both the need for friends and habitual patterns of socializing helped to keep alive many friendships that were far from ideal. A friend was only human, they said, and therefore partook in the common frailties of the species.

The women seldom engaged in quarreling and criticizing each other. Why not? Fundamentally it was connected with their reliance on each other for some aspects of their definitions of themselves. When a friend criticized her behavior, a woman felt that her identity had been questioned, that her view of herself that she had expected her friend to uphold had been sullied. The disapproval of some behavior or ideas that were important enough to fight over was a frontal attack on the inner core of herself. If she was seen as less than she wanted to appear in the eyes of her friend, she felt that she was no longer such a good and attractive person in her own eyes. Her friend's estimation of her worth was crucial to the maintenance of the person she believed she was. As we have seen, friends hesitated to tell another woman to change or correct her behavior. Putting herself in her friend's position, she wondered whether she would be misunderstood, whether her friend would regard the criticism as a hostile attack instead of a well-meaning gesture. Was it worth the inevitable confrontation and the hurt? Would it cause a rupture in a valued relationship? As the women said in various ways, "If we quarrel, how will we make up?" More basically, they were saying, "If she hurts my feelings about myself that much, how can I ever trust her with myself again?"

The women in the friendship study adhered to a norm of graciousness in the conduct of their friendships. They were slow and indirect about conveying dissatisfaction with a long-term relationship because they were sensitive to the possibility of hurting another woman's feelings. As for bringing a friendship to an end, the etiquette seemed to demand a gradual pace of disengagement, the notion being that the other woman should be given ample opportunity to adjust to breaking off the relationship. In that way both of the friends would be less likely to suffer the pain and embarrassment accompanying sudden withdrawal or an open quarrel.

When friends had succeeded in developing especially close and varied bonds holding the relationship together, they created an invisible web of connections that was not casually broken. The cultural ideals about faithfulness in friendship also buttressed the relationship, and members of their immediate social networks occasionally served as mediators when problems arose between intimates. But the maintenance of a friendship between middle-class women lay largely in their own hands.[3] The women in the study said that, while their relationships with their friends were not perfect, they valued what was good about them and counted on keeping them. The alternative was loneliness. The women understood that friendships required attention, that friends were sometimes boring, disappointing, or exasperating, and that everything would not be pleasing about these relationships all the time. This understanding of the nature of friendship tempered somewhat their idealized versions of friendship and helped them to come to terms with the realities of being and having an adult friend.

NOTES

1. For additional material on the impact of separation and divorce on women's friendships, see Robert S. Weiss, *Marital Separation*, New York: Basic Books, 1975; Lynne C. Halem, *Separated and Divorced Women, Westport, CT: Greenwood Press, 1982, especially pp. 150-52; Robert R. Bell, Worlds of Friendship*, Beverly Hills, CA: Sage, 1981.

2. Concerning the stability of various types of personal relationships, George McCall wrote: "Both romance and friendship . . . rest primarily on bonds of attachment, benefit-dependability, and rather tentative commitments; and these forms are well known to be easily and frequently broken off." George J. McCall, "Becoming Unrelated: The Management of Bond Dissolution," in Steve Duck, ed., *Personal Relationships 4: Dissolving Personal Relationships*, New York: Academic Press, 1982, p. 215.

3. In some instances where the women belonged to close-knit networks of friends, they volunteered or were asked to help ease strains between friends. For an analysis of the social pressures exerted by surrounding social networks, see John J. La Gaipa, "Rules and Rituals in Disengaging from Relationships," in Duck, ed., *Personal Relationships 4*. Most of the time, however, the friendships were conducted on a one-to-one basis without direct outside interference. Robert Paine wrote that "the making and breaking of friendships in our society is largely a matter of personal choice that is beyond social control." Robert Paine, "In Search of Friendship: An Exploratory Analysis of 'Middle-Class' Culture."*Man*, 1969, p. 514.

CHAPTER 6

Postscript

Question: How many friends would you say you have?

Answer: Let's see. I have three friends. Is that enough?

Having friends—good enough friends or a sufficient number of them—was important to the middle-class American women interviewed for the Adult Women's Friendship Project. The testimony of these women indicated that they wanted very much to have either one close friend—a real confidante—or a few very good friends, not just a circle of sociable companions. At the same time they recognized the virtue of having a variety of acquaintances for passing the time enjoyably and keeping themselves amused. Most of them said that they put a good deal of stock in their friendships and spent a considerable amount ot time, thought, and energy cultivating them, whenever and if that was possible to do in the course of their crowded schedules. Some spoke with real regret about how little time they had to devote to their friends. "It is frustrating," one woman commented, "to realize perfectly well that you are missing out on something you could enjoy but everything else seems to have to get done before you fit in some private hour or so with a good friend." Another woman put it this way: "I sort of feel it in my bones that I need to have friends for my own well-being. That sounds selfish, I realize. But I have this kind of intuitive sense that my friends round out my life in ways nobody else really can do, not even my husband, not my children, not my mother, not anybody else I am related to." The women without friends said they felt lonely.

In view of these comments on the significance of friendship it was surprising to discover that the social research on the subject of adult friendship has tended to downgrade friendship as an important aspect of middle-class women's lives. The quality and intensity of our interviews threw doubt on these findings, as did the evidence of the determined search the women in the sample had undertaken to find friends. This evidence was spelled out in the stories of the efforts the women had made to make new friends and to hold on to old ones. For example, they had tried engaging in activities and in joining organizations with a specific purpose of finding among the members some women who could be transformed from acquaintances into friends. At least for this sample of women, friendships loomed large as an important aspect of their lives.

The rise of what appears to be a growing consciousness of a need to develop and maintain a circle of friends deserves explanation. It seems to come about in part from the increasing problematic world of middle-class women—a world that is undergoing rapid and confusing change. Stable marriages can no longer be taken for granted: on the contrary, their impermanence is taken for granted. Families move, move again, and move still once more—diminishing the social and emotional support once supplied by kin and old friends. About half the labor force consists of women, many of whom have developed some independence from the nuclear family. Women now live longer, live a larger and larger portion of their lives without children at home and without husbands present.

Beyond being just one of the optional relationships in life then—to be chosen or rejected on the basis of convenience and whim—friendship may be making a bid for first place or rivaling first place as a provider of the intimacy and support needed by every woman at some period of her life. Indeed, for the ever-growing numbers of American women who are alone or live alone—the never married, separated, childless, divorced and widowed, the empty-nested and stranded in the suburbs or city apartments—

friendship may not be just a dispensable frill, but a necessity for a woman's well-being. The absence of a support system provided by friends can have serious consequences: it can be detrimental not only to her emotional stability, but also to her physical health.

FRIENDSHIP AS AN ACCOMPLISHMENT

The creation of a personal network of friends is no easy task. One of the stereotypes about women is that they possess a natural capacity for promoting positive social-emotional relationships. They are regarded as having the ability to make friends easily and almost effortlessly. The fact is that making friends and being a friend is a complex process, requiring a good deal of initiative and persistence. Although it may seem to "just happen," actually it involves much planning and purposeful organization. As jobs increasingly dominate middle-class women's time, there are many constraints on the availability of possible partners. Appointments for meeting with friends must be made; busy schedules must be dovetailed (Kurth 1984). It has been pointed out that "making friends with someone is a skilled performance in the same sense (as) driving a car or playing tennis. . . . All depend on knowing what to do next to bring the object or person nearer the desired state, then doing it, then observing the effect" (Cook 1977, 320). In other words, success at making new friends comes from positive efforts and sophisticated skills that are put into practice repeatedly throughout a lifetime of experience. Looked at this way, friendship is an accomplishment rather than merely the natural consequence of the meeting of two persons with similar backgrounds and shared attitudes.

In real life, then, friendships do not happen automatically, even though all the demographic variables and common values would predict compatibility between two strangers. It is particularly noticeable that energies must be mobilized to form new friendships and maintain them. If, for personal or structural reasons, either the dedication to cultivating new friends is lacking or the skills are not put into play, loss of friendship may be so extensive that the single person becomes socially isolated or spouses have virtually no friendships except with each other and immediate family members. Evidence indicates that this is more apt to happen to men than to women (Crawford 1977; Levinson 1978).

Because changing residences and leaving communities periodically go hand in hand with being middle class, women in the middle class are repeatedly faced with the need to create individual patterns of living that have not been structured by family and other long-term associations.[1] With each successive uprooting, women not only organize a household into a home for their families (or, if alone, for themselves), but also, in due course, take active steps to try to reconstitute at least some semblance of a small community of caring people with whom they can gradually interact face to face on a personal basis. They undertake a search for new friends. Even though they may continue to keep in touch with some of their friends from former suburbs and home cities by telephone, mail, and occasional visits, these long-distance relationships are not sufficient. Some local friends are needed. Although some women accumulate a few friends from each place they have lived, most of the middle-class people who are geographically mobile allow a majority of their old friendships to lapse when they move to a new area and begin once again to cultivate new friends (Bell 1968; Pahl and Pahl 1971). The loss of the former and particularly deep attachments is not readily sloughed off by women who leave their devoted friends with begrudging regrets. They are the ones who protest against having to give up the network of ties they have worked to establish. Still the proportion of old to new friends diminishes with years of residence in a new location (Hess 1972).

American women of the migratory middle class have suffered from the depersonalizing effects of urbanization and residential mobility. In making the transitions from one place of residence to another the women are always forced to put together a new scaffolding around which they can build a network of social relations for themselves and their families. In these activities of taking down old frameworks and constructing new ones, they are the prototypical modern members of the family unit, the ones who are confronted with rapid social changes affecting their personal lives. Although they may acquire the skills and orientations to enable them to accomplish the tasks of reconstruction through repeated training, they do the usual female work of managing the social and emotional welfare of the family members without the traditional support of their mothers, sisters, aunts, cousins, and female in-laws. They straddle the old and the new world, not necessarily giving up the strong attachments to relatives living elsewhere, but often becoming estranged from their more traditional way of life through the broadening access to the fruits of upward mobility. The burdens of the throw-away, tear-down, remodel, redecorate society are shouldered by them without much help from the social institutions, which are slow to supply new forms of organized social life. The disturbances to connections in their surroundings are felt by women in the privacy of their individual homes, apartments, and offices. Mobility breaks up the fabric of life, and it is the women who go about mending it and making it whole again. Doing it alone, they do not always succeed. Women do the job of establishing a small society around them with various degrees of effectiveness and in a number of configurations that may change over a lifetime.

It is ironic that when moving, the migrants, with fewer economic resources, suffer less from isolation and absence of structure that do the middle class (Fischer 1977). For example, the Appalachian people who went to the cities in search of work, and the Italian immigrants to America were received in particular cities and enclaves by the kin and friends who preceded them. Such networks determined the choice of their destination, with personal communication between the earlier migrants and those in the home village preparing the way for the latest entrants. These people may have come either individually or in a family, but they followed "chains of migration" that assured them connections with people who would help them settle into the strange new setting. Anthropologists were surprised to discover how well Africans from tribal lands adjusted to urban life, even though they were apt to be scattered throughout the cities in mixed neighborhoods. Even when faced with all the strangeness of an industrial labor market, new living arrangements, and bureaucratic regulations, they were helped by their tribesmen to make a remarkably quick and good accommodation to the abrupt transition from agricultural to urban life.

For middle-class Americans, adjustments to transitions are handled on a much more individualistic basis. The part women play in establishing the small social worlds for themselves and their families involves ongoing efforts to make friends and maintain them. Their search for friends can be detected most easily when something happens to disturb, in some way, the equilibrium of their private social networks. It is not only their own residential mobility that can upset the supply of personal relationships needed for a satisfying environment. Friends of long standing may leave the area. Work, family, and health changes of many sorts, new interests and activities, and new stages in the family life cycle may precipitate the process of finding new friends by breaking up the old personal order.

The community of friends that many middle-class women create almost out of whole cloth is a notable human accomplishment. Always honored in fable and history between men, friendship is an achievement of women that has never been equally celebrated. Our view is that competence at making and keeping friends among women is something to be admired, is something that is learned, and is of great significance in their lives.

THE WOMEN'S MOVEMENT AND FRIENDSHIP

Some have suggested that the women's movement helped create a social climate in which female friendships re-emerged as significant ties after a period of decline. In part, through its ideology of sisterhood, it is said, the movement altered the way women felt about and acted with other women.[2] It taught women to honor their commitments to their friends and to be supportive of other women. Of course the impact of a social movement is not necessarily understood by the people it affects. In the sample of middle-class women interviewed for the Adult Women's Friendship Project, only two of the women said the women's movement had any direct influence on their friendships.[3] Both of these women had taken part in movement activities with women who eventually became close friends. A married woman in her early forties, who had returned to a local community college to finish her undergraduate degree, recalled that she had accepted an invitation to join a consciousness-raising group composed of women of about the same age. About this experience, she said:

I didn't know what to expect at the beginning. I thought I was going to be afraid to say anything, but it turned out to be so easy. We would meet at somebody's house one night a week at 9 o'clock and stay until the wee hours, and talk and drink wine. We talked about everything, we had no agenda. It would just start and go on and on. I'll never forget it. It was so incredible. The five of us felt very close, and three of us still see each other a great deal.

The other respondent who referred to the movement as a prime source of her friendships had been an anti-war activist in high school and had then become a leader in the women's movement on a state university campus. She talked about the impact of the ideal sisterhood on her attitude toward women in general and her own network of friends in particular. "They are all sisters in my life, but of my close friends in the movement, to me these women are my world, and I am their world." She described some characteristics of this special group of friends:

First of all, they are all feminists, and I think that has to do with a certain part of feminism that requires trust. That is because we took real chances. You do work with rape, you make lots of enemies. You make lots of friends, but you make lots of enemies too. You do work on abortion, you make lots of enemies. It's the real McCoy. I don't mean to be melodramatic, but you need to trust people's discretion when you are organizing and all these people have done political work. I think we all developed a need for trust and I think we developed the ability to be public people, but both intimate and private at the same time.

This woman went on to make the connection between working in the movement and establishing friendships with coworkers:

I really would argue that our friendship was through the women's movement, although probably all of us had the inclination to be friends in the beginning. It's interesting. I hadn't thought about it before, but I think that's what happened. Of the three ways women organize, I am convinced they organize best around child care, rape, and abortion, and rape is the best for making friends. My friends were on some nasty assault cases and we were all involved in encouraging (institutions) to respond to that in a thoughtful way and that was really the source of our firm friendship because we did this thing together.

By addressing this issue openly, they took risks together—risks to their jobs and to their reputations as faculty members. "The risk," she said, "was in becoming visible. I think of feminism as being for equalilty and justice. But that's not the public version of feminism: the mild version is shrill, and the extreme version is that feminism is destructive of the family and the social order. That's the way it is viewed. So we took these risks together, and I think, for my friends and I, we found that adversity brings you together." The interviewer interjected a question: "It's almost like a war?" The answer: "It's certainly almost a war, but it's not as grim as that all the time. That's not how I would characterize what brought us together. We also had a great deal of fun together. We had lots of fun. We went to dinner together and all that stuff."

Despite the absence of any reference to the women's movement on the part of most women in their friendship interviews, it is our hunch that the women's movement has influenced the conduct of women's friendships in many subtle ways. Little is known about the effects of feminist ideas on the personal relationships of women in all areas of their lives. Until more studies have been made, any conclusions are premature.

THE NEW BREED

Among our respondents there were women—most of whom were in their thirties and forties but some of those in their fifties and sixties—who put their friendships with other women at the core of their lives. They consciously sought out and went to great lengths to maintain a circle of close friends and friendly acquaintances with whom they planned regular occasions for getting together. What was strikingly different about their choices of how to spend their time away from work was that they did not always prefer to be with a man. They tended not to seek either the company or the protection that males were thought to provide as much as their predecessors had done. Many of the unmarried were not actively seeking a marital partner. As single, divorced, or widowed women, they did not feel particularly vulnerable or anxious because of their unmarried status.

In general, what we are calling the New Breed were professionals or some sort of middle-level managers. They had long since left home and were financially independent. Some were upwardly mobile; others came from affluent families. Some were married or living with a man; some were not. A few had children at home. Some had grown children. Most had moved many times. They were well educated and appeared to be, for the most part, dominant personalities. They tended to be assertive, intensely competitive, and highly ambitious people. They had taken the measure of their colleagues—both men and women—and were confident of their own abilities.

The "reference groups" of these women—the people whose perspectives they shared and used to judge themselves—were sometimes a circle of friends and acquaintances in the same profession or business. Thus one woman in the sample talked at length about the fact that her "best friends," including men, were in the same profession and that she saw them regularly at various types of meetings around the country. She had no self-doubts about her future: she was going to be one of the most accomplished in her field and "go to the top." She probably wouldn't marry but got pleasure and support from her "best friends" in the profession, whom she saw at least several times a year.

As they moved ahead in their careers, these women had built up a network of friends along the way, some of whom they thought would be friends for life. As one particularly articulate woman said, "When I say I love them and they love me, (with) the kind of support and understanding, communication, and integration that transcends place and time, I know that these two women and my friend Jane, we will be friends till the day we die." A manager in her early forties who had been living with a man for five years said, "My relationship with Jim is fine and good but who knows how long it will last. My friendship with Marilyn is forever. I am certain it will never end."

Not all the women in these friendship circles were so close, by any means. Sometimes competition and jealousy eroded the relationships. Nevertheless they did things for each other. Assistance was asked for and granted, whether a recommendation for a new position, help with personal emergencies, or the sharing of information of various sorts. The women told of many instances of both small and large favors that were readily done for one another.

Many of the New Breed women earned substantial salaries that allowed them to purchase property—a city condominium or a house on the suburban fringe, in the exurbs, or in a smaller city. Most of them had a good deal of disposable income after regular expenses, but this was not true of all of them. Financial resources were much slimmer for two types of the women in the New Breed group: these were the younger women in their early thirties who were still in the lower ranks of their occupations and the single and divorced women who were raising children alone. Of those who were in good financial shape, their affluence permitted them to spend money on themselves and on doing things with each other, such as frequently dining out, going to the theater, movies, museums, art shows, exercise spas, sports events, lectures, and each other's parties, and traveling to visit each other. Some of them took vacation trips together.

The New Breed women were busy people with high energy levels. They worked hard and enjoyed the fruits of their labor with equal intensity. Although quite a few of them had a serious or a casual relationship with a man, they did not sit at home and wait for men to invite them out. Instead they planned their own recreation, most of which included friends, both men and women, on similarly tight schedules. This meant that they made arrangements to fill in many of the hours, outside of those committed to work and to personal and household maintenance, with some kind of social engagements with friends. They also balanced their social life with solitary pursuits, such as reading and keeping up with the news, reviews, and cultural trends. They were readers and critics of what they read and saw. If not always trendsetters, they recognized what was new and interesting early on.

Among other things, there seemed to be an emphasis on the intellectual as well as the emotional quality of their relationships. The people chosen as friends were not only personable and attractive and liked for themselves, but they were "interesting," "challenging," and "knew a lot." Rarely included as their friends were people who did not contribute to either their amusement or their development. The fact that a few of these women referred to some of their acquaintances as "boring" simply highlighted, by comparison, the qualities they preferred their associates to possess. While necessarily having to keep up with developments in their own fields of specialty, they also tried to have a working familiarity with what was happening in at least some aspects of the intellectual, cultural, and artistic life of the nation. Of course there was a wide range among them in how well they succeeded in accomplishing this goal, and they tended to be stronger in some areas of interest and weaker in those of less concern to them. They frequently specialized in their cultural interests and involvements: some, for example, in the ballet and theater, while others were aficionados in current literature or the visual arts. Because they lived and worked at the centers of these developments, it was not unduly taxing on them to stay well informed about the latest trends. They counted on each other informally for staying abreast, and they sought and gave advice to each other about many things, including the practical problems of living, such as difficulties with people at work and the advisability of a career change.

By and large, their friendships seemed to be rich in that both parties brought to the relationships a variety of backgrounds and experiences. When asked to say what they liked about being with their friends, they stressed the good times they had together rather than all the indirect benefits that went along with their association. They had "fun" together, and they expected their friends to fill their leisure hours with amusing conversation and join them in relaxing and stimulating diversions.

Because the women we talked with had moved around the country a number of times, starting in early adulthood, when they went away to college and sometimes to graduate school, they might have fitted into that unflattering portrait of corporate wives who have been described as superficial in their attachments to the people they lived among temporarily before their husbands got better jobs. That might have been true of those women who were expected to act as adjuncts to the corporate family in the 1950s, but the New Breed women all spoke of having kept a number of friends living elsewhere. They valued these friendships and, if possible, wanted to sustain some of them. Within the limits of the time and energy available, they appeared to have selected a few friends to stay in touch with long distance. In some instances business travel and attendance at professional meetings and conventions allowed them to renew their earlier close relationships on an occasional face-to-face basis, and some of them used their vacations for reunions. The threads connecting some friendships remained unbroken if the women continued communicating and had occasional opportunities to meet and talk and renew the tie in person. Some women literally had friends strewn around the world. As one woman described friendship at a distance: "I didn't have any close friends here. I had all these other friends and I used to spend a lot of time on the phone and my airline bills were pretty high. I worked on this project and the project paid for my trips back to the Midwest. I didn't make any money out of it, but it did cover five trips to . . . where I would be with my friends."

The New Breed women who were married or had live-in lovers were steadfast about keeping their friends and doing things with them. Their limited free time was spent not just in being with their husbands/lovers and families and socializing with other couples. Instead they planned to see their friends so that there would be occasions for private conversations, and when that was difficult to work into their schedules, they kept in touch by telephone—and often these calls would last for several hours. These friendships were frequently not shared with their spouses, but conducted separately from the marital/lover pairs. The independence of such friendships from the men was in sharp contrast with the pattern of socializing reported in earlier studies (Lopata 1975). The women were no longer tailoring their friendships to whether they would turn into couple socializing. "I no longer think of whether I'll like her husband or she'll like mine as a basis for the beginning of a new friendship," explained a professional woman now living at home with two children. "Aside from everything else, I have always found it impossible to expect that all four members of two couples will take to each other. I prefer it would work that way. And I think Joe and I tend to be attracted to the same types of people. But when you get all the permutations in temperament, interest, and so forth of four people, it is not so easy to bring off. In our case it rarely does. I can remember some disastrous evenings when I tried to get a friend and her husband acquainted with my husband."

The key problems in the development and maintenance of the New Breed friendships were similar to those discussed throughout the book. A shortage of time loomed as the largest problem. Enough time for the cultivation of friendships, the commitments to the husband, lover, or children, and of course the demands of the work place were always at issue. The difficulties encountered in maintaining her friendships were described by a woman in the advertising business who had remained single until she was twenty-nine years old and had developed a group of good female friends—very supportive ones. After she was married and had a baby, she opened an advertising agency in partnership with one of these close friends. Running her own business in addition to rearing her baby meant she had little free time. "I'm on the go all day long, and at night I have to be home with my husband and baby. Something has to suffer. Too often it's friendship." But she was determined not to give up her old friends. "After all, my friends were there for me when there was no husband, no baby, and I didn't have my own business." Typically she associated with these friends in social groups as couples and as families but felt that was not enough to maintain the intimacy they once had. "Friends need you to be alone with them sometimes, need you to give them your undivided attention . . . and you need the same thing from them" (Wolfe 1983, 23). This emphasis on preserving the integrity of the friendship meant that some privacy was required in the form of a long conversation at lunch, a walk together alone for an hour, an extended time to talk in an undistracted setting to allow the needed catching up and continuity of thought and feeling to take place.

Possibly our sample was too small and selective to say anything conclusive about this New Breed of women and their friends. The outlines of these friendships were still being filled out. However difficult it seemed to be to keep these friendships going, and whatever new shapes they were taking in the characteristic ebb and flow of such relationships, this group of business and professional women seemed to be making successful efforts at creating and maintaining a circle of friends. These friends were regarded not as a luxury, but as a necessity they were unwilling to give up. Some of these women had husbands or lovers and children. But in contrast with the findings derived from earlier studies of friendship among adults, friendships among some of these women were not second best to their bond with the members of their nuclear families. The ascendancy of friendship in the lives of this group of women may turn out to be a harbinger of things to come.

NOTES ON THE FUTURE

There is every indication that the factors that have encouraged a new emphasis on the value of friendship among women will continue to operate.[4] It is predicted that a growing proportion of women will continue to enter the labor force, with a higher percentage of women in the professional and executive ranks. Middle- and upper-middle-class women will continue to be well educated, marry later, have small families, and live longer. Many will have both independence and adequate financial resources of their own. They will change residence frequently over a lifetime and be separated geographically from their relatives. Some will not marry at all or, after divorce, not marry again. It is plausible to think that these trends will reduce the exclusive reliance on the family for close personal relationships. At the same time they will create a need for strong and enduring attachments outside the family circle.

For many women who are separated from their relatives, friends will assume some of the characteristics of family members in the sense that they have become the source of unquestioning support in time of need. In their interviews some of the women reported seeing a friend through a personal crisis, assuming responsibilities that relatives might be expected to take. It was clear that some women got from their friends that which they could earlier have counted on getting only from their families. In fact some of the younger women said they would turn by choice to a friend, rather than to a relative, for help or counsel because they thought their problems would be better understood and considered more objectively and dispassionately by a friend. The friend seems to have become the confidante of choice over the mother, sister, or some other relative.

Demographic trends underscore the importance of friendship in the lives of older women. Although both men and women are living longer and living longer in better health, women live longer and are healthier, on the whole, than men. Often geographically separated from their adult children, surviving widows stay alone in their houses or apartments or move to the Sun Cities, retirement villages, or nursing homes. Their associations with other women are sometimes the only option for social life and emotional support. Even if they keep former friendships alive by visits, phone, or mail, and even if they are in regular contact with their grown children, the practical help and give-and-take of everyday life often comes from the person living in the next house or apartment or the adjacent bedroom (Adams 1985-86).

As women grow older they will benefit from the interpersonal skills they have developed at making close friendship bonds. These later years bring dramatic changes, such as retirement, moving to another community, and death of a spouse. For the middle- and upper-middle-class woman, "her pattern of shared social activities . . . with other women of like status prior to widowhood constitutes a 'reservoir' of social opportunities for companionship and emotional closeness" (Blau 1961, 435). Studies of friendships among the elderly indicate that some strong nonfamily ties are indispensable to their emotional and physical health. Relationships with grown children, however frequent and intense, do not compensate for a lack of a confidante. In fact, the possession of just one close friend can serve as a barrier against the depression and loneliness that often accompany the last decades of life (Lowenthal and Haven 1968).

A number of women in our sample were giving thought to the role their friends would play in their lives in the very long term. Whether or not they carry out arrangements to live with one other female friend or a group of female friends, they predictably will outlast all but a small percentage of the men in their own age cohort. Older women who are widows, divorcées, and never marrieds will have to live either alone, with adult children or other relatives, or in housing for the elderly. Alternatively, they can plan ahead to live with or near their old friends. Whether or not these retirement plans materialize, the skills at making long-lasting friendships and cultivating new relationships will stand middle-class women in good stead for the quality of life in late adulthood. As a fifty-year-old lawyer put it, "I'm investing in friendship and expect to collect regular dividends throughout my life. I watch my investment carefully but don't expect to shift it into another account because I already know it's well managed, solid, and reliable for the long haul. My friends are my social security and insurance policy combined."

NOTES

1. About 17 percent of the U.S. population changed residences during the year between 1980 and 1981. Approximately 38 percent of those who were twenty to twenty-four years old and 31 percent of those who were twenty-five to twenty-nine years old lived in a different house one year earlier. Higher education increased the likelihood of geographical mobility, with college graduates apt to move more frequently than high school graduates. Among the population twenty-five years old and over, 16 percent with four or more years of college moved between March 1980 and March 1981. U.S. Bureau of the Census. "Geographical Mobility, March 1980 to March 1981." *Current Population Reports*, Series P-20, No. 377. Washington, D.C.: Government Printing Office, 1983.

2. Seiden and Bart pointed out that the women's movement encouraged women to take their female friendships more seriously, not to treat them as mere pastimes. "The movement supported them in conceptualizing the value of friendships." Anne M. Seiden and Pauline B. Bart, "Woman to Woman: Is Sisterhood Powerful?" in Nona Glazer-Malbin, ed., *Old Family/New Family*, New York: Van Nostrand, 1975, p. 193.

3. In his interviews, Bell had similar responses when he asked women about the importance of the women's movement for their friendships. "Very few said it had any direct influence. However, most did say they had always had close relationships with other women. A number of them also reported that the movement had helped make them more aware of the value and significance of their female friendships. For our respondents the women's movement had been supportive rather than causative in their friendships." Robert R. Bell, *Worlds of Friendship*, Beverly Hills, CA: Sage, 1981, p. 73.

4. Speculation about the future will profit from studies of the past in which the conditions supporting friendship are documented. But historians have paid little attention until recently to friendships between women. However, the new scholarship devoted to women's history has documented a rich heritage of female friendship in earlier periods. The letters and diaries of the women who migrated to isolated homesteads on the Great Plains revealed how much they suffered when they were cut off from the network of female friends who had been a sustaining part of daily life "back home" (Stansell 1976, 92).

In the settled New England towns and cities the women of the prosperous classes developed a "newly self-conscious and idealized concept of female friendship. This ideal became a subject of their conversations, reading, reflection, and writing" (Cott 1977, 160). These women frequently turned to each other for the affection and intimacy so often missing from their marriages. "An abundance of manuscript evidence suggests that eighteenth- and nineteenth-century women routinely formed emotional ties with other women. Such deeply felt same-sex friendships were commonly accepted in American society. Indeed, from the late eighteenth century through the mid-nineteenth century, a female world of varied and yet highly structured relationships appear to have been an essential aspect of American society. These relationships ranged from the supportive love of sisters, through the enthusiasms of adolescent girls, to the sensual avowals of love by mature women. It was a world in which men made but a shadowy appearance" (Smith-Rosenberg 1975, 19).

Avowals of affection between women, which sound strange to modern ears, were routinely expressed and casually accepted in their day (Easton 1979). A letter written to Susan B. Anthony by Elizabeth Cady Stanton put into words the tender and supportive quality of the relationship between these leaders of the women's suffrage movement. Elizabeth wrote to her friend Susan: "So closely interwoven have been our lives, our purposes, and experience that, separated, we have a feeling of incompleteness—united, such strengths of self-assertion that no ordinary obstacles, difficulties, or dangers ever appear insurmountable" (Rossi 1973, 389).

Bibliography

Adams, Bert N. "Isolation, Function, and Beyond: American Kinship in the 1960s." *Journal of Marriage and the Family*, 1970, pp. 575-99.

Adams, Rebecca G. "Emotional Closeness and Physical Distance Between Friends: Implications for Elderly Women Living in Age-Segregated and Age-Integrated Settings." *International Journal of Aging and Human Development*, 1985-86, pp. 55-76.

Aldous, Joan. "Intergenerational Visiting Patterns: Variations in Boundary Maintenance as an Explanation." *Family Process*, 1967, pp. 235-51.

Allan, Graham A. *A Sociology of Friendship and Kinship*. London: Allen and Unwin, 1979.

Altman, Irwin, and D. A. Taylor. *Social Penetration*. New York: Holt, Rinehart and Winston, 1973.

Atkinson, J. W. *Motives in Fantasy, Action and Society*. Princeton, N.J.: Van Nostrand, 1958.

Backman, C. W., and P. F. Secord. "The Effect of Perceived Liking on Interpersonal Attraction." *Human Relations*, 1959, pp. 379-84.

Bardwick, Judith. "The Dynamics of Successful People." In Dorothy G. McGuigan, ed., *New Research on Women*. Ann Arbor, Mich.: University of Michigan Press, 1974.

Bell, C. R. *Middle Class Families*. London: Routledge and Kegan Paul, 1968.

Bell, Robert R. *Worlds of Friendship*. Beverly Hills, Calif.: Sage, 1981.

Bensman, Joseph, and Robert Lilienfeld. *Between Public and Private: The Lost Boundaries of the Self*. New York: Free Press, 1979.

Berardo, Felix. "Kinship Interaction and Communication among Space-age Migrants." *Journal of Marriage and the Family*, 1967, pp. 541-54.

Bernard, Jessie. *The Future of Marriage*. New York: World, 1972.

———. *The Female World*. New York: Free Press, 1981.

Bernikow, Louise. *Among Women*. New York: Harper and Row, 1981.

Berscheid, Ellen, and E. H. Walster. *Interpersonal Attraction*. Reading, Mass.: Addison-Wesley, 1968.

Bigelow, Brian, and John J. La Gaipa. "Children's Written Descriptions of Friendship: A Multi-dimensional Analysis." *Developmental Psychology*, 1975, pp. 857-58.

Birnbaum, Judith A. "Life Patterns and Self-esteem in Gifted Family-oriented and Career-committed Women." In Martha Mednick, Sandra Tangri, and Lois Hoffman, eds., *Women and Achievement*. Washington, DC: Hemisphere, 1975.

Blau, Zena Smith. "Structural Constraints on Friendship in Old Age." *American Sociological Review*, 1961, pp. 429-39.

———. *Old Age in a Changing Society*. New York: Franklin Watts, 1973.

Bott, Elizabeth. *Family and Social Networks: Roles, Norms, and External Relationships of Ordinary Urban Families*. New York: Free Press, 1971.

Brown, B. Bradford. "A Life-Span Approach to Friendship: Age-Related Dimensions of an Ageless Relationship." In Helena Z. Lopata and David Maines, eds., *Research in the Interweave of Social Roles: Friendship*. Greenwich, Conn.: JAI Press, 1981.

Brown, Linda Keller. *The Woman Manager in the United States: A Research Analysis and Bibliography*. Washington, DC: Business and Professional Women's Foundation, 1981.

Byrne, Donn. *The Attraction Paradigm*. New York: Academic Press, 1971.

Candy, Sandra G., Lillian E. Troll, and Sheldon C. Levy. "A Developmental Exploration of Friendship Functions of Women." *Psychology of Women Quarterly*, 1981, pp. 456-72.

Chelune, Gordon J., Joan T. Robison and Martin J. Kommor. "A Cognitive Interactional Model of Intimate Relationships." In Valerian J. Derlega, ed., *Communication, Intimacy, and Close Relationships*. New York: Academic Press, 1984.

Cook, Mark. "The Social Skill Model and Interpersonal Attraction." In Steve W. Duck, ed., *Theory and Practice in Interpersonal Attraction*. New York: Academic Press, 1977.

Cott, Nancy. *The Bonds of Womanhood*. New Haven, Conn.: Yale University Press, 1977.

Crawford, M. "What Is a Friend?" *New Society*, June 20, 1977, pp. 116-17.

DeCharms, Richard, and Gerald H. Moeller. "Values Expressed in American Children's Readers: 1800-1950." *Journal of Abnormal and Social Psychology*, 1962, pp. 136-42.

Derlega, V. J., and A. L. Chaikin. "Privacy and Self-Disclosure in Social Relationships." *Journal of Social Issues*, 1977, pp. 102-15.

Dickens, Wenda J., and Daniel Perlman. "Friendship Over the Life-Cycle" In Steve Duck and Robin Gilmour, eds., *Personal Relationships. 2: Developing Personal Relationships.* New York: Academic Press, 1981.

Dion, K. K., E. Berscheid, and E. H. Walster. "What Is Beautiful Is Good." *Journal of Personality and Social Psychology*, 1972, pp. 285-90.

Douvan, Elizabeth. "Interpersonal Relationships: Some Questions and Observations." In George Levinger and Harold L. Raush, eds., *Close Relationships.* Amherst, Mass.: University of Massachusetts Press, 1977.

Douvan, Elizabeth, and Joseph Adelson. *The Adolescent Experience.* New York: Wiley, 1966.

Duck, Steve. "Personality Similarity and Friendship Formation: Similarity of What, When?" *Journal of Personality*, 1973, pp. 543-58.

———. *The Study of Acquaintance.* Westmead, England: Saxon, 1977a.

———. "Tell Me Where Is Fancy Bred: Some Thoughts on the Study of Interpersonal Attraction." In Steve W. Duck , ed., *Theory and Practice in Interpersonal Attraction.* New York: Academic Press, 1977b.

———. "Toward a Research Map for the Study of Relationship Breakdown." In Steve Duck and Robin Gilmour, eds., *Personal Relationships. 3.* New York: Academic Press, 1981c.

Duck, Steve, ed. *Personal Relationships. 4: Dissolving Personal Relationships.* New York: Academic Press, 1982.

Duck, Steve, and Robin Gilmour, eds. *Personal Relationships. 1: Studying Personal Relationships.* New York: Academic Press, 1981a.

Duck, Steve, and Robin Gilmour, eds. *Personal Relationships. 2: Developing Personal Relationships.* New York: Academic Press, 1981b.

Duck, Steve, and Robin Gilmour, eds. *Personal Relationships. 3: Personal Relationships in Disorder.* New York: Academic Press, 1981c.

Easton, Barbara. "Feminism and the Contemporary Family." In Nancy F. Cott and Elizabeth H. Pleck, eds., *A Heritage of Her Own: Toward a Social History of American Women.* New York: Simon and Schuster, 1979.

Ellison, Ralph. *The Invisible Man.* New York: Random House, 1952.

Epstein, Cynthia. "Law Partners and Marital Partners: Strains and Solutions in the Dual-Career Family Enterprise." *Human Relations*, 1971, pp. 549-64.

Festinger, Leon, et al. *Social Pressures in Informal Groups.* New York: Harper and Brothers, 1950.

Fischer, Claude S. "Network Analysis and Urban Studies." In Claude S. Fischer et al., *Networks and Places: Social Relations in Urban Settings.* New York: Free Press, 1977.

Fischer, Claude S. et al. *Networks and Places: Social Relations in Urban Settings.* New York: Free Press, 1977.

Franck, Karen A. "Friends and Strangers: The Social Experience of Living in Urban and Non-Urban Settings." *Journal of Social Issues*, 1980, pp. 52-71.

Frank, Francine, and Frank Anshen. *Language and the Sexes.* Albany, N.Y.: State University of New York, 1983.

Giele, Janet Zollinger, ed. *Women in the Middle Years: Current Knowledge and Directions for Research and Policy.* New York: Wiley-Interscience, 1982.

Gilligan, Carol. *In a Different Voice: Psychological Theory and Women's Development.* Cambridge, Mass: Harvard University Press, 1982.

Glazer-Malbin, Nona, ed. *Old Family/New Family.* New York: Van Nostrand, 1975.

Goffman, Erving. "On Face-Work: Analysis of Ritual Elements in Social Interaction." *Psychiatry*, 1955, pp. 213-31.

———. *The Presentation of Self in Everyday Life.* Garden City, N.Y.: Doubleday, 1959.

———. *Interaction Ritual: Essays in Face-to-Face Behavior.* New York: Anchor Books, 1967.

Gouldner, Helen P. "The Organization Woman: Patterns of Friendship and Organizational Commitment." Ph.D. dissertation, University of California, Los Angeles, 1959.

———. "Dimensions of Organizational Commitment." *Administrative Science Quarterly*, 1960, pp. 468-90.

Gray, Francine du Plessix. "On Friendship." *Bryn Mawr Alumnae Bulletin*, Spring 1979, pp. 2-3.

Halem, Lynne C. *Separated and Divorced Women.* Westport, Conn.: Greenwood Press, 1982.

Handy, C. "Going Against the Grain: Working Couples and Greedy Occupations." In Rhona Rapoport and Robert Rapoport, eds., *Working Couples.* New York: Harper and Row, 1978.

Hartup, W. W., J. A. Glazer, and R. Charlesworth. "Peer Reinforcement and Sociometric Status." *Child Development*, 1967, pp. 1017-24.

Hatfield, Elaine. "The Dangers of Intimacy." In Valerian J. Derlega, ed., *Communication, Intimacy, and Close Relationships*. New York: Academic Press, 1984.

Hendrick, D., and S. R. Brown. "Introversion, Extroversion, and Interpersonal Attraction." *Journal of Personality and Social Psychology*, 1971, pp. 250-58.

Hennig, Margaret, and Anne Jardim. *The Managerial Woman*. New York: Pocket Books, 1978.

Henry, Jules. *Culture Against Man*. New York: Vintage Press, 1965.

Hess, Beth B. "Friendship." In Matilda White Riley, Marilyn Johnson, and Anne Foner, eds., *Aging and Society*. Vol. 3, *A Sociology of Age Stratification*. New York: Russell Sage, 1972.

———. "Sex Roles, Friendship and the Life Course." *Research on Aging*, 1979, pp. 494-515.

Holmes, Donald J. *Psychotherapy*. Boston: Little, Brown, 1972.

Hunter, J. "Persistence of Local Sentiments in Mass Society." In D. Street, ed., *Handbook of Contemporary Urban Life*. San Francisco: Jossey-Bass, 1978.

Jacobson, David. "Fair-weather Friend: Label and Context in Middle-class Friendships." *Journal of Anthropological Research*, 1975, pp. 225-34.

Johnson, Michael P. "Social and Cognitive Features of the Dissolution of Commitment to Relationships." In Steve Duck, ed., *Personal Relationships. 4: Dissolving Personal Relationships*. New York: Academic Press, 1982.

Jong-Gierveld, Jenny. "Loneliness and the Degree of Intimacy in Interpersonal Relationships." In Robin Gilmour and Steven Duck, eds., *The Emerging Field of Personal Relationships*. Hillsdale, N.J.: Lawrence Erlbaum Associates, 1985.

Jourard, S. M. *Self-disclosure: An Experimental Study of the Transparent Self.* New York: Wiley-Interscience, 1971.

Kanter, Rosabeth Moss. *Men and Women in the Corporation*. New York: Basic Books, 1977.

Kanter, Rosabeth Moss, and Barry A. Stein, eds. *Life in Organizations: Workplaces as People Experience Them*. New York: Basic Books, 1979.

Kelvin, Peter. "Predictability, Power and Vulnerability in Interpersonal Attraction." In Steve Duck, ed., *Theory and Practice in Interpersonal Attraction*. New York: Academic Press, 1977.

Kleiman, Carol. *Women's Networks*. New York: Lippincott and Crowell, 1980.

Komarovsky, Mirra. *Blue-collar Marriage*. New York: Random House, 1962.

Kramarae, Cheris. *Women and Men Speaking*. Rowley, Mass.: Newbury House, 1981.

Kurth, Suzanne B. "Friendships and Friendly Relations." In George J. McCall, ed., *Social Relationships*. Chicago: Aldine, 1970.

———. "Social and Structural Constraints on Nonromantic Voluntary Relationship Formation." Paper presented at International Conference on Personal Relationships, July 1984, Madison, Wisconsin.

La Gaipa, John J. "A Systems Approach." In Steve Duck and Robin Gilmour, eds., *Personal Relationships 2: Developing Personal Relationships*. New York: Academic Press, 1981.

———. "Rules and Rituals in Disengaging from Relationships." In Steve Duck, ed., *Personal Relationships 4: Dissolving Personal Relationships*. New York: Academic Press, 1982.

Lazarsfeld, Paul F., and Robert K. Merton. "Friendship as Social Process: A Substantive and Methodological Analysis." In Monroe Berger, Theodore Abel, and Charles H. Page, eds., *Freedom and Control in Modern Society*. New York: Octagon, 1954.

Lever, Janet. "Sex Differences in the Games Children Play." *Social Problems*, 1976, pp. 478-87.

Levinger, George, and Harold L. Raush, eds. *Close Relationships*. Amherst, Mass.: University of Massachusetts Press, 1977.

Levinson, Daniel J., with Charlotte N. Darrow, Edward B. Klein, Martha R. Levinson, and Broxton McKee. *The Seasons of a Man's Life*. New York: Alfred A. Knopf, 1978.

Liebow, Elliott. *Tally's Corner*. Boston: Little, Brown, 1967.

Lofland, Lyn H. *A World of Strangers: Order and Action in Urban Public Space*. New York: Basic Books, 1973.

———. "The 'Thereness' of Women: A Selective Review of Urban Sociology." In Marcia Millman and Rosabeth Moss Kanter, eds., *Another Voice: Feminist Perspective on Social Life and Social Science*. New York: Anchor Books, 1975.

Lopata, Helena Z. *Widowhood in an American City*. Cambridge, Mass.: Schenkman, 1973.

———. "Couple-Companionate Relationships in Marriage and Widowhood." In Nona Glazer-Malbin, ed., *Old Family/New Family*. New York: Van Nostrand, 1975.

———. *Women as Widows*. New York: Elsevier, 1979.

———. "Friendship: Historical and Theoretical Introduction." In Helena

Z. Lopata and David Maines, eds., *Research in the Interweave of Social Roles: Friendship*. Greenwich, Conn.: JAI Press, 1981.

Lopata, Helena Z. and David Maines, eds. *Research in the Interweave of Social Roles: Friendship*. Greenwich, Conn.: JAI Press, 1981.

Lorber, Judith. *Women Physicians: Careers, Status, and Power*. New York: Tavistock, 1984.

Lowenthal, Marjorie Fiske, and Clayton Haven. "Interaction and Adaptation: Intimacy as a Crucial Variable." *American Sociological Review*, 1968, pp. 20-30.

Lowenthal, Marjorie Fiske, Majda Thurnher, and David Chiriboga. *Four Stages of Life: A Comparative Study of Women and Men Facing Transitions*. San Francisco: Jossey-Bass, 1975.

McAdams, Dan P. "Human Motives and Personal Relationships." In Valerian J. Derlega, ed., *Communication, Intimacy, and Close Relationships*. New York: Academic Press, 1984.

McCall, George J. "Becoming Unrelated: The Management of Bond Dissolution." In Steve Duck, ed., *Personal Relationships. 4: Dissolving Personal Relationships*. New York: Academic Press, 1982.

McCall, George J., and J. L. Simmons. *Identities and Interactions*. New York: Free Press, 1966.

McClelland, D. C., ed. *Studies in Motivation*. New York: Appleton-Century-Crofts, 1955.

Maccoby, Eleanor E., and Carol N. Jacklin. *The Psychology of Sex Differences*. Stanford, Calif.: Stanford University, 1974.

Mann, Judy. "Remember the Time. . . . " *The Washington Post*, May 29, 1985.

Mayer, John E. "The Self-Restraint of Friends: A Mechanism in Family Transition." *Social Forces*, 1957, pp. 230-38.

Miell, Dorothy. "Strategies in Information Exchange in Developing Relationships: Evidence for a Unique Relational Context." Paper presented at the International Conference on Personal Relationships, July 1984, Madison, Wisconsin.

Milgrim, Stanley. "The Small World Problem." *Psychology Today*, May 1967, pp. 61-67.

Miller, Jean Baker. *Toward a New Psychology of Women*. Boston: Beacon Press, 1976.

Millman, Marcia, and Rosabeth M. Kanter, eds. *Another Voice: Feminist Perspective on Social Life and Social Science*. New York: Anchor Books, 1975.

Newcomb, Theodore M. *The Acquaintanceship Process*. New York: Holt, Rinehart and Winston, 1961.

Packard, Vance. *A Nation of Strangers*. New York: David Mckay, 1972.

Pahl, J. M., and R. D. Pahl. *Managers and Their Wives.* Harmondsworth, England: Penguin Books, 1971.

Paine, Robert. "In Search of Friendship: An Exploratory Analysis in 'Middle-Class' Culture." *Man,* 1969, pp. 505-24.

Parlee, Mary Brown. "The Friendship Bond." *Psychology Today,* 1979, pp. 43-45, 49-50, 53-54, 113.

Pleck, Joseph H. "The Work-Family Role System." *Social Problems,* 1977, pp. 417-27.

———. "Husband's Paid Work and Family Roles." In Helena Z. Lopata and Joseph Pleck, eds., *Research in the Interweave of Social Roles: Families and Jobs,* Vol. 3. Greenwich, Conn.: JAI Press, 1983.

Powers, Edward A., and Gordon L. Bultena. "Sex Differences in Intimate Friendships in Old Age." *Journal of Marriage and the Family,* 1976, pp. 739-47.

Rainwater, Lee, Richard P. Coleman, and Gerald Handel. *Workingman's Wife: Her Personality, World and Life Style.* New York: McFadden-Bartell, 1961.

Rapoport, Rhona, and Robert Rapoport. "Three Generations of Dual-Career Family Research." In F. Pepitone-Rockwell, ed., *Dual-Career Couples.* Beverly Hills, Calif.: Sage, 1980.

Rapoport, Rhona, and Robert Rapoport, eds. *Working Couples.* New York: Harper and Row, 1978.

Rawlins, William K. "Openness as Problematic in Ongoing Friendships: Two Conversational Dilemmas." *Communication Monographs,* 1983, pp. 1-12.

Reisman, John M. "Adult Friendships." In Steve Duck and Robin Gilmour, eds., *Personal Relationships 2: Developing Personal Relationships.* New York: Academic Press, 1981.

Riesman, David. *The Lonely Crowd.* New Haven, Conn.: Yale University Press, 1950.

Rodin, Miriam J. "Non-engagement, Failure to Engage, and Disengagement." In Steve Duck, ed., *Personal Relationships 4: Dissolving Personal Relationships.* New York: Academic Press, 1982.

Rokeach, Milton, ed. *The Open and Closed Mind.* New York: Basic Books, 1960.

Rossi, Alice S. "A Feminist Friendship: Elizabeth Cody Stanton (1815-1902) and Susan B. Anthony (1810-1906)." In Alice B. Rossi, ed., *The Feminist Papers.* New York: Columbia University Press, 1973.

Rubin, Lillian B. *Women of a Certain Age: The Midlife Search for Self.* New York: Harper and Row, 1979.

———. *Just Friends: The Role of Friendship in Our Lives.* New York: Harper and Row, 1985.

Rubin, Zick. *Children's Friendships*. Cambridge, Mass.: Harvard University Press, 1980.

Salamon, Sonya. "Family Bounds and Friendship Bonds: Japan and West Germany." *Journal of Marriage and the Family*, 1977, pp. 807-20.

Schlenker, Barry R. "Identities, Identifications, and Relationships." In Valerian J. Derlega, ed., *Communication, Intimacy, and Close Relationships*. New York: Academic Press, 1984.

Schneider, D. J., A. H. Hastorf, P. C. Ellsworth. *Person Perception*. Reading, Mass.: Addison-Wesley, 1979.

Schofield, William. *Psychotherapy: The Purchase of Friendship*. Englewood, N.J.: Prentice-Hall, 1964.

Secord, S. F., and C. W. Backman. *Social Psychology*. New York: McGraw-Hill, 1964.

Seiden, Anne M., and Pauline B. Bart. "Woman to Woman: Is Sisterhood Powerful?" In Nona Glazer-Malbin, ed., *Old Family/New Family*. New York: Van Nostrand, 1975.

Selman, Robert L. *The Growth of Interpersonal Understanding*. New York: Academic Press, 1980.

Shulman, Norman. "Life-Cycle Variations in Patterns of Close Relationships." *Journal of Marriage and the Family*, 1975, pp. 813-21.

Simmel, Georg. *The Sociology of Georg Simmel*, translated by Kurt H. Wolff. New York: Free Press, 1950.

Smith, Ralph E., ed. *The Subtle Revolution: Women at Work*. Washington, D.C.: The Urban Institute, 1979.

Smith-Rosenberg, Carroll. "The Female World of Love and Ritual: Relations Between Women in Nineteenth-Century America." *Signs*, 1975, pp. 1-28.

Stansell, Christine. "Women on the Great Plains 1865-1890." *Women's Studies*, 1976, pp. 87-98.

Stolorow, R., and G. Atwood. *Faces in the Cloud: Subjectivity in Personality Theory*. New York: Jason Aronson, 1979.

Stroebe, W., C. A. Insko, V. S. Thompson, and B. D. Layton. "Effects of Physical Attractiveness, Attitude Similarity and Sex on Various Aspects of Interpersonal Attraction." *Journal of Personality and Social Psychology*, 1971, pp. 79-91.

Stueve, C. Ann, and Kathleen Gerson. "Personal Relations Across the Life-Cycle." In Claude S. Fischer et al., eds., *Networks and Places: Social Relations in Urban Settings*. New York: Free Press, 1977, pp. 79-98.

Sussman, Marvin B., and Lee Burchinal. "Parental Aid to Married Children: Implications for Family Functioning." *Marriage and Family Living*, 1962, pp. 320-32.

Thorne, Barrie, and Nancy Henley, eds., *Language and Sex: Difference and Dominance*. Rowley, Mass.: Newbury House, 1975.

Troll, Lillian E. "The Family in Later Life: A Decade Review." *Journal of Marriage and the Family*, 1971, pp. 263-90.

Trower, Peter. "Social Skill Disorder." In Steve Duck and Robin Gilmour, eds., *Personal Relationships 3: Personal Relationships in Disorder*. New York: Academic Press, 1981.

Turner, Ralph H. "Moral Judgment: A Study in Roles." *American Sociological Review*, 1952, pp. 70-77.

———. *Family Interaction*. New York: Wiley, 1970.

U.S. Bureau of the Census. "Money Income and Poverty Status of Families and Persons in the United States, 1979." Series P-60, No. 125, Advance Report. Washington, D.C.: Government Printing Office, 1981.

———. "Geographical Mobility, March 1980 to March 1981." *Current Population Reports*, Series P-20, No. 377. Washington, D.C.: Government Printing Office, 1983.

———. *We, The American Women*. Washington, D.C.: Government Printing Office, 1984.

Verbrugge, Lois M. "The Structure of Adult Friendship Choices." *Social Forces*, 1977, pp. 576-97.

Weiss, Lawrence, and Marjorie Fiske. "Life-Course Perspectives on Friendship." In Marjorie Fiske Lowenthal, Majda Thurnher, and David Chiriboga. *Four Stages of Life: A Comparative Study of Women and Men Facing Transitions*. San Francisco: Jossey-Bass, 1975.

Weiss, Robert S. "The Fund of Sociability." *Transaction*, July-August 1969, pp. 36-43.

———. *Loneliness: The Experience of Emotional and Social Isolation*. Cambridge, Mass.: Massachusetts Institute of Technology, 1973.

———. *Marital Separation*. New York: Basic Books, 1975.

Whyte, William H., Jr. *The Organization Man*. New York: Simon and Schuster, 1956.

Wolfe, Linda. "Friendship in the City." *New York*, July 18, 1983, pp. 20, 22-28.

Women's Bureau. *Time of Change: 1983 Handbook of Women Workers*. Bulletin 298. Washington, D.C.: Government Printing Office, 1984.

Wright, Derek. "On Friends." *New Society*, June 1970.

Wright, Paul H. "Self-referent Motivation and the Intrinsic Quality of Friendship." *Journal of Social and Personal Relationships*, 1984, pp. 115-30.

Index

About the Authors

HELEN GOULDNER is Dean of the College of Arts and Science and Professor of Sociology at the University of Delaware. She is the author of the prize-winning study *Teachers' Pets, Troublemakers and Nobodies: Black Children in Elementary School* (Greenwood Press, 1978), and co-author of *Modern Sociology*.

MARY SYMONS STRONG is an editorial consultant and the former editor of *Transaction Magazine*. She is the co-editor of *Sociological Realities*.